A Table in the Tarn

A Table in the Tarn

ORLANDO MURRIN

Living, Eating and Cooking in Rural France

Published in 2008 by Stewart, Tabori & Chang
An imprint of Harry N. Abrams, Inc.

Text copyright © 2009 by Orlando Murrin and Peter Steggall
Photographs copyright © 2009 by Jonathan Buckley
Plan of the Manor © 2009 by Neil Gower

Library of Congress Cataloging-in-Publication Data:

Murrin, Orlando.
  A table in the Tarn / Orlando Murrin.
      p. cm.
  Includes index.
  ISBN 978-1-58479-762-3
  1. Cookery, French. 2. Cookery--France--Tarn River Valley. 3.
Le Manoir
de Raynaudes. I. Title.
  TX719.M878 2009
  641.5944'737--dc22

                                2008033392

The text of this book was composed in Cezanne, Scala and
Scala Sans.

Printed and bound in China

10 9 8 7 6 5 4 3 2 1

HNA ▇▇▇▇
harry n. abrams, inc.
a subsidiary of La Martinière Groupe

115 West 18th Street
New York, NY 10011
www.hnabooks.com

Tongue orchids (*Serapias lingua*) in the meadow in
front of the Manoir.

For my mother and father, Patsy and Pat, who brought me up to appreciate the finer things in life.

Contents

The Cast

ORLANDO MURRIN: fanatic cook and gardener, threw in highly desirable job as editor of *BBC Good Food* to open a posh b&b in rural France. Impetuous but single-minded, he runs the Manoir's kitchen, garden and "shop."

PETER STEGGALL: ex-IT director in financial services, he is the Manoir's front man, looking after reservations, guests, housekeeping, staff, cellar and money matters. Cool and charming, he is equally at home calculating tax returns and suggesting something fruity to drink with tonight's duck.

THE BONNÉS: one-time owners of the Manoir, now nearest neighbors. GILBERT is a fanatic—of wood (from sawing beams to whittling ornamental mushrooms), grafting fruit trees (by the phases of the moon) and the accordion. Twinkly MAURICETTE divides her time between potager and kitchen, regaling passers-by with rapturous cooees and jars of *cerises à l'Armagnac*.

MONIQUE: housekeeper. Superwoman with a wardrobe to outdo Joseph, she has a nervous disposition and is easy victim of practical jokes, e.g. tapping on her window while she is ironing and pretending to be a fox. Enemy number one: stains. Enemy number two: creases.

Clockwise, from above: Orlando Murrin and Peter Steggall, The Bonnés, Caro, Ginette and Michel Regourd and red setter Sam, Mme Guilhen and Monique.

CARO: deputy cook. Unflappable pro with flash background in recipe development and food photography, sent by God to live a village away. Food stylist for this book—no one can touch her on dust-fine chopping of herbs or applying gold leaf to after-dinner chocs. Apparently inscrutable, she is the Manoir's main source of local, international and TV (e.g. *Neighbours, Prison Break*) gossip.

BENOÎT: waiter, works at the Manoir during his holidays from Toulouse business school to improve his English. Proud owner of . . . NAPOLI: ten-year-old Spitz who is unsuspectingly being fattened on Manoir leftovers.

THE REGOURDS: affable farming couple living in the old Raynaudes schoolhouse. GINETTE works her vegetables full time (the household is self-sufficient). MICHEL and red setter SAM cut the Manoir hay each June. A local councillor, Michel has inside track on Monestiès politics.

OTHER VILLAGERS include Mme Cayre (Georgette), Mme Dauzats (a.k.a. the Wealthy Widow), M. et Mme Cluzel, Mme Guilhen, M. et Mme Gloriès.

The Story starts

in a loft apartment overlooking the City of London, and moves to the Tarn *département* in southwest France—specifically Raynaudes (nickname "The Hamlet Time Forgot"), near the village of Monestiès ("Sleepy Hollow").

THE STORY OF THE MANOIR

House-hunting

OUR FIRST GLIMPSE OF THE MANOIR DE RAYNAUDES was through freezing drizzle, at dusk on New Year's Eve 2001. It had been a long, depressing day of viewings, and as we came down the hill from the main road, I could pick out a lake, a stand of poplars and the tall, elegant shape of a house. It was the thirty-sixth property we had looked at over the course of seven visits to the area during late summer, autumn and early winter. We had seen the lot—farmhouses half buried in mud, twee converted barns, d-i-y nightmares and dilapidated châteaux. At one turreted wreck, the door was opened by a distressed woman in her fifties who insisted no, her home was not for sale, her estranged husband would have to murder her first.

We had put in an offer on a gleaming white stone house among vineyards near Gaillac, only to find the owner (if indeed he was the owner) would only sell for cash. And we nearly fell for a six-story mansion in thick woodland near Castres (whose widow proprietor bore an uncanny resemblance to Cilla Black)—until we counted 56 windows, all needing replacing (to say nothing of the 112 flaky shutters that went with them).

I remember that we were on the point of giving up the game. It had all sounded so simple—we just wanted a house suitable to run as a b&b. We had a list of requirements and preferences, but nothing that exacting. It mattered not if it was in a village, town or in the country, as long as it

Looking south from the Manoir (previous spread), an ancient pear tree, weighed down with mistletoe and summer hangout for a family of hoopoes.

had a pleasant aspect. Any age or condition, but preferably with a bit of character. As for location, we had started our search in Cordes, the most beautiful of the bastide towns in the Albi area, and visit by visit, thrown the net wider.

Moments later we curled around the lake and a pair of ducks splashed into the water. Through the gray I could make out a small orchard, then in front of us—it may have been a trick of the light—was the imposing Manoir, dramatically backlit with silver. A tiny minaret set in the peak of the gable seemed for a second to glitter. We made our way to the stone gateway and clanged the bell outside the huge wooden *portail*.

No one knows the origins of the Manoir, but the current house was built in about 1860 in the bastide style. The word *bastide* is particular to southern France and has romantic connotations of Cathars and crusades. Bastide towns were defensive "new towns" built in the 1100s and 1200s, consisting of concentric circles of walls and dwellings around a central marketplace. There are no less than fifty-six of them in the Tarn *département* (of which Albi is the capital). Bastide farmhouses were also defensive, built around a central courtyard with all doors and windows facing inwards, entered by one or two gated archways. The Manoir has the characteristic courtyard and the arches, but thanks to the safer age in which it was built, a graceful abundance of doors and windows facing outwards.

What we could not know that grim evening was the sheer beauty of the view those windows enjoy: an unfolding panorama of pasture, meadows, copses, hills and—in the far distance—the glint of the snowcaps of the Pyrenées. Nor, because it promptly started to snow, could we step out of the house into the field beyond: a sheltered, sunny dip where we would later build our garden.

Instead we embarked on a listless tour of the house. The sitting room, with chilly exposed stone walls, was cut in half by an oddly shaped arch, giving a *bierkeller* atmosphere. A lean-to kitchen extruded into the courtyard. It was hard to say if the staircase was the remains of the original, or a half-hearted replacement. It led to a maze of corridors and bedrooms, and up another wooden ladder into the attic. In one corner of the attic we noticed a triangle of round holes in the wall, long cemented up. Every self-respecting house

in the area has a *pigeonnier* or pigeon loft, either built in, as here, or detached—in which case they are often quite fanciful, half-timbered or on stilts. This was, however, enough to be going on with.

We trudged muddily back to the car. With the sense of anticlimax I believe explorers experience when, after weeks of trekking through ice and snow, they finally reach the North Pole, Peter asked me: "What do you think?"

"Exactly on brief," I replied. "I was beginning to think we were asking the impossible, but it's everything we're looking for."

"So if we're serious about all this, there's nothing to stop us. Go for it?"

"Go for it."

Our first planting was an avenue of twenty-four lime trees (variety 'Greenspire') approaching the house. In early summer it fills the air with sweet scent.

Long before I ever visited this area I was a fan of Paula Wolfert's *The Cooking of Southwest France*, in which she describes a buttery brioche with a layer of fragrant melted cheese in the middle, made in the town of St. Affrique near Roquefort. Made many times and subtly adapted, this has become one of the Manoir's signature dishes.

Roquefort brioche

Enough for 8–10, cut into wedges like a cake

FOR THE BRIOCHE DOUGH

⅓ cup warm milk

2 tsp fresh yeast (see note on page 220 if using dried)

2 cups bread flour

1 tsp salt

1 egg plus 1 yolk

½ tbsp sugar

1½ sticks (12 tbsp) unsalted butter, at room temperature

TO BAKE

5 tbsp Roquefort cheese, crumbled

½ cup Cantal or Cheddar cheese, grated

1 egg, beaten

You will need a large fluted brioche pan or deep 8-inch cake pan, greased

Start a day ahead. This recipe is involved but the time spent actually doing things is minimal, so make this when you are planning to be in the kitchen anyway and can keep an eye on progress. Brioche dough is fantastically sticky, so I keep my hands out of it.

Put the milk and the yeast in the bowl of a food mixer and mix briefly. Add the flour and salt, lay a tea towel over the mixer to prevent a flour dust-storm, and mix with dough hook till moistened. Add the egg, yolk and sugar till mixed, scraping the sides with a spatula. Add the butter in about 12 chunks, allowing each to be incorporated before adding the next. Mix on medium speed for 10 minutes, to a sticky, smooth, glossy batter. Turn into a large plastic box or bowl, cover and leave in a warm place till doubled, 1–3 hours. (The time varies according to temperature and your yeast.)

Without removing from the box or bowl, use a bench scraper or spatula to pull up the sides of the dough and deflate it. Refrigerate for 2 hours, stirring down 2 or 3 times. Cover the surface with plastic wrap and refrigerate overnight.

About four hours before serving, turn out the dough (it will be solid) onto a well-floured surface. Press out just over half to form a rough 8 inch circle and fit into the base of the greased pan, nudging the sides up to form a narrow, slightly raised border. Sprinkle the Roquefort and half the Cantal evenly over the base, leaving the border bare. Divide the remaining dough into about a dozen pieces and, using floured hands, roll into balls. Arrange on top of the dough, pressing to flatten them slightly (they will not at this point

cover the surface completely). Cover with a sheet of greased foil and leave to rise for 2–3 hours, till roughly doubled again. Glaze the balls and rim generously with egg (you will not need it all), sprinkle with the remaining Cantal and bake for about 12 minutes at 425°F (400°F convection), then, without opening the oven, turn it down to 350°F (325°F convection) for a further 12–15 minutes. If the brioche gets too brown towards the end of its cooking time, cover with a sheet of foil. Check with a skewer to ensure it is fully cooked through. Cool for 10 minutes on the baking sheet, invert on to a rack, then set the right way up on the rack to continue cooling. Serve warm.

Renovation

ONE OF MY MOST TREASURED PHOTOGRAPHS was taken at the *acte de vente* in February 2002, a singularly French ceremony at which a property purchase is completed, and which made us official owners of Le Manoir de Raynaudes. Against the background of the fusty office of a provincial *notaire*, it shows Peter, me, Maître Lafage (a *notaire* being a rank above mere *monsieur*), and the Bonné family from whom we bought the house and land—Gilbert and his wife Mauricette, their son Jean-Claude and his wife Françoise.

The *notaire*'s job is to ensure that everyone understands exactly what is being bought and sold, to which end he reads out, word by word, the seemingly interminable contract, and the owner of the bar on the other side of Pampelonne village square, who speaks English, paraphrases. Everyone present then initials every page, and signs the last page with the words *lu et approuvé* (read and approved). There is much courteous shuffling back and forth of the papers.

Gilbert Bonné was born in the house next door to the Manoir, and Mauricette has lived there since she married him at eighteen. Life for French country folk was tough, physical work. The women's job was to produce food—which meant tending the potager, poultry, a pig and perhaps a few rabbits—while the men worked the land. At midsummer everyone worked around the clock to bring in the harvest, and if you had a bad back or were injured, you carried on regardless. After years of such labor, it is hardly surprising that many of our country neighbors are now stooped and bent by painful arthritis.

The front terrace of the Manoir, where guests are served dinner under the catalpa tree, accompanied by the singing of nightingales.

Through scrimping and saving, Gilbert and Mauricette bought a piece of land with the Manoir in the middle of it. Their elder son Jean-Claude made a brave start on renovating it—clearing out the house and outhouses (*dépendances*), putting a new roof on the barn and prettying up the terrace with a few shrubs—before the decision was taken to sell.

The moment we had the keys, I could not wait to pounce on the garden, which after a London roof terrace held limitless possibilities. The thirteen acres around the Manoir included an ancient footpath, a coppice of 100 young oaks with a secret pond, a lake, stream and cherry orchard, as well as ten acres of gently sloping meadow, which is virgin land, never treated with fertilizers or pesticides.

Knowing how builders love to park cement mixers in flower beds and tread on plants to keep their boots dry, my first efforts were well away from the house. The cherry orchard, which then consisted of a dozen rather overgrown trees, was full of dead wood, and the dam below the lake had been used as a dump. There were two or three trees to be felled in the copse, and the hedges had not been trimmed for several years.

These jobs were tackled during holidays and snatched weekends, because of course Peter and I were still based in London. We anticipated that the renovation would take about two years, and that we would fulfill our dream of opening for business in four or five. Anyone who has ever tackled a long-distance renovation will know what an agony of waiting life seemed at that period. We woke up every morning dreaming of knocking holes in walls and digging out tree stumps, but instead had to slog through the London traffic to go to our offices. In the end, we drastically telescoped our timetable.

One of our first decisions, and in retrospect the most influential of the whole project, was choosing our architect. Peter had for a couple of years known a talented young Tel Aviv architect and interior designer called Ofir Asiass. As Ofir had relatively recently qualified, he eked out his living between architectural assignments by teaching design and working as cabin crew for El-Al. Whenever a flight brought him to London, we would talk long into the night about joists, skirting boards, wiring circuits and paint finishes.

His plans for the Manoir were strikingly original. In the barn, for example, Ofir came up with a dazzling design for four double-height "duplex" apartments, open to the beamed roof, with galleried bedrooms and chandeliers. Blending the old and new elements of the Manoir posed him no problem. "We make the modern look modern, and make good the old. And here where we're putting the study, we front it with 27 square yards of aluminium and glass. We don't pretend."

Knowing that we wanted the swimming pool to be tucked away rather than plonked ostentatiously in front of the house, Ofir cut it entirely into the slope behind the house and surrounded it with a "beach" of washed pebbles and palm trees. In the main house, he remodeled the catacomb-style arch to make a large open salon, and designed a

The hub of Manoir life is the central courtyard, decorated in summer by boxes of lush brugmansia, and dominated by the aluminium and refractive-glass study.

glittering staircase of steel, wire and wood, the like of which the local (lady) blacksmith, commissioned to make and install it, had never seen. The first floor was turned into two huge bedroom suites, with two more on the second floor. All this in a style of—if such a thing exists—understated minimalism.

We had read or heard many horror stories of French renovation projects that went wrong—indeed whole books have been written about them. When you are dealing with old buildings there are so many unknown elements that there is always going to be the odd nasty surprise, and we had our share. Making good the barn, for example, turned out to be a delicate and extremely expensive procedure. Like

The swimming pool was cut into the slope behind the open barn, a shady space for reading and relaxing.

most farm buildings in the area, it is made of a mixture of mud and layers of stone incapable of supporting modern floors, ceilings or indeed a solid roof. The solution was to build an entirely new, independent concrete frame inside the barn to support the living accommodation, at the same time as keeping the charming exterior—sandy, mellow and weatherworn—intact.

It soon also became apparent that our original budget had to be torn up and rewritten. It was not that the various contractors went over their original estimates—if they said it would be 480 euros to plumb in a shower, that was the price we were charged. But as we increasingly discovered, that estimate covered a fraction of the job, and in subsequent days or weeks it would be joined by an estimate for joining the plumbing to the hot-water system, then the cold-water system, then the drains system, then for putting the base beneath the shower, then for sealing the shower base, then for putting the piece of wood at the front. (To say nothing of tiling, filling, finishing and decorating around said shower—which involved estimates from three other contractors.)

In my frustration at these ever-mushrooming estimates, I remember stamping my feet over the downstairs lavatory. "When I say we want a light in here, I mean we want a wire from the mains, we want a bit of wire on which to attach a light, we want a bit of wire to a switch, we want a switch—all attached, all working, all one estimate. Please."

Certain elements of the renovation proceeded better than expected, and certain contractors (or artisans, as they prefer to be called in France) went the extra mile. It seems much the same wherever you do building work—for every dodgy plumber you find a life-enhancing electrician, for every lazy roofer you find a genius bricklayer. Our team was entirely French, project-managed with mixed success by a Frenchman and Englishman, a role we took over ourselves in the later stages.

Stars of our show were young electrician Vivian (as long as you kept him off the subject of his reptile collection), Alain Lafage, the dapper carpenter (who let off surplus energy by shouting at his apprentice), Thierry Barreau, the gentleman tiler (who jotted wine recommendations for us on the flaps of tile boxes).

So, slowly, the Manoir began to come together. We were delighted by the refurbished sitting room and bedrooms, which looked so light, fresh, elegant—so *French*. The grandeur of the newly cobbled courtyard, with its colossal new oak doors at each end and fuzzy-pink-blossomed albizzia freshly planted in the middle. The gracious sweep of the gravel terrace in front of the house, which Ofir insisted be a massive 3¼ yards wide. Later we were also to discover how well the buildings work together, the orangerie as a cool retreat for evening drinks, the open barn (aka the hangar) a shady place to sit when it gets too hot by the pool, the courtyard as the hub of Manoir life.

If this were a television program, however, the producer would demand the bad moments as well as the good. For me, one has to be when the plumber turned on his new central-heating system in the main house without apparently having tested any part of it. I will never forget the shouts from around the house as the artisans in various rooms found themselves suddenly sprayed with water, and how—panic stricken—the plumber raced from room to room hacking holes in freshly decorated walls and ceilings to try and seal the dozen or so leaks. And later when the plumber (coincidentally the same person) turned on his new hot-water system in the main house without apparently having tested any part of it, and failed to notice the water pouring over the crates containing all our possessions and furniture, including my 1892 Blüthner grand piano, until it was an inch deep around them.

Another forgettable time was just before we opened for business. We had accepted a booking for the end of May 2004, at which point—whatever it took—all work would be finished and all contractors off-site. Of course, by April there were literally hundreds of small jobs that had not been finished. Contractors either refused to do them because they had not been estimated for (the old story) or they said were the responsibility of another contractor.

Would we tackle another renovation project in the future? It is said that it is a self-protective human trait to forget pain and remember pleasure, but our final desperate weeks of round the clock contractor-bashing, finishing jobs off, correcting botches, filling holes and covering up mistakes will stay with me for a very long time.

And, of course, we would do it again tomorrow.

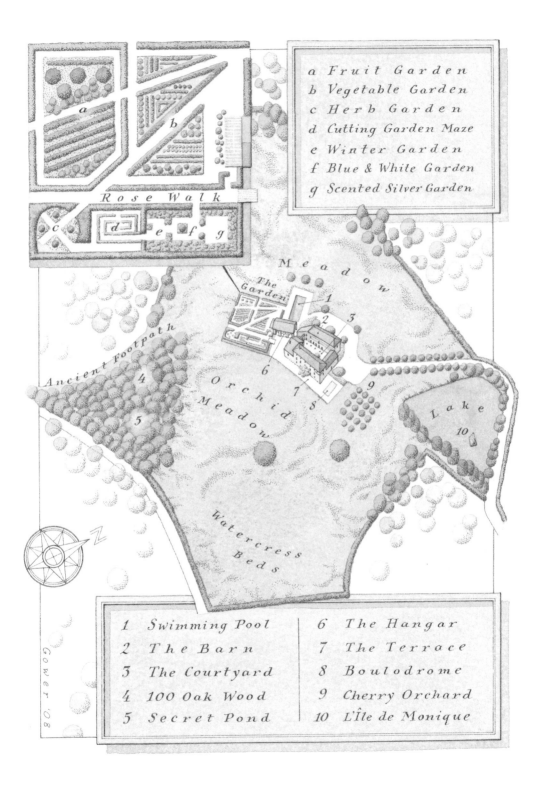

a Fruit Garden
b Vegetable Garden
c Herb Garden
d Cutting Garden Maze
e Winter Garden
f Blue & White Garden
g Scented Silver Garden

Rose Walk

Meadow

The Garden

Ancient Footpath

Orchid Meadow

Lake

Watercress Beds

Gower '08

1 Swimming Pool
2 The Barn
3 The Courtyard
4 100 Oak Wood
5 Secret Pond

6 The Hangar
7 The Terrace
8 Boulodrome
9 Cherry Orchard
10 L'Île de Monique

Our *femme de ménage* Monique professes to love all food, but her special favorites are the French country dishes she was brought up with. I first met *chou farci* in Jane Grigson's *Charcuterie and French Pork Cookery*, and make it in the heart of winter.

Stuffed cabbage à la Monique

Serves 4 gourmands

1 Savoy cabbage (the crinkly kind)

1¼ pounds Toulouse sausages, skins removed, or sausage meat

1 egg, beaten

3 slices of bread made into crumbs, or ¼ cup fresh bread crumbs

chopped fresh herbs, such as thyme and parsley

about 1¼ cups stock or mixture of stock and wine

You will also need kitchen string and scissors

Choose a pot into which the cabbage will fit comfortably but not too spaciously. Fill it with salted water and bring to the boil. Discard any damaged cabbage leaves and carefully cut out most of the core with a small pointed knife. Slide into the water and boil for 5 minutes, then drain until cool enough to handle. Rinse the pot.

Put the cabbage on a board cut-side down, string and scissors to hand. Put the stuffing ingredients in a bowl (sausage, egg, bread, herbs) and season generously but do not mix yet.

Now get your hands in. Carefully peel back the outermost leaf of cabbage, then work round to the next leaf and do the same. Continue working round the cabbage, turning it as you go—the order is obvious. Try not to tear the leaves. They will get stiffer and less malleable as you work toward the center. Stop when all you are left with is a small yellow cone of leaves.

Pause for a second to admire the extraordinary flowerlike beauty of a humble cabbage.

Mix the stuffing ingredients with your hands. Take the equivalent of a good spoonful and press around the base of the cone. Pull up the three or four leaves around it and press lightly together so they stay in place. Now continue by putting a spoonful or so of sausage mixture at the very base of each leaf, pulling it back up to where it started, working your way round, slowly returning the cabbage to its original form. As you go, it will get harder to keep the cabbage in shape. You may run out of sausage meat by the time you get to the final leaves, or have to put in extra to use it all up, but it does not matter.

Tie the cabbage up snugly, knotting at the top, so you can lift it out using the strings. Bring the stock to the boil in the pot you were using earlier. Lower in the cabbage and season lightly. Scrunch up a piece of parchment paper so it is easy to shape, and push down over the cabbage to keep it moist. Bring to the boil again and put on a lid.

Bake for 3–4 hours at 300°F (275°F convection), basting occasionally, by which time the cabbage will be meltingly tender when prodded with a knife and have filled the kitchen with tempting savory aromas. Check the seasoning of the sauce.

This is rustic cooking at its best but it is not a glamorous dish. Ideally, serve direct from the pot. If not, carefully lift it out using the string, supporting it underneath with a wide spatula, into a wide bowl. Pour over the sauce.

Remove the string and serve in lavishly thick wedges with the sauce.

RAYNAUDES SECRET

Do not rush this dish. Opening out the cabbage takes a little time, and it needs the full three hours' cooking (or four if convenient). You can thicken the sauce if you wish by boiling to reduce, or with *beurre manié*— mash together 1 tbsp butter and 1 tbsp flour then drop bit by bit into the boiling sauce, whisking constantly, until thickened to your liking.

The Move

BUT THIS IS LEAPING AHEAD. For the first eighteen months of building work at Raynaudes, Peter and I were still living in London, making the most of everything the capital had to offer—recitals at the Barbican and Festival Hall, films, even guided city walks—knowing that at some point in the future we would be living a much more rural lifestyle.

To free up capital we sold our flat in Shoreditch, from which Peter had been able to walk each morning to his job off Bishopsgate. Disappointingly, we had to accept a low offer that barely covered the money we had spent on it, and the buyer's solicitor tried to knock us down further at the last minute by trumping up some story about a medieval right of way involving the shared car park in the basement. If that is what London property transactions have come to, we thought, we are better off out of it.

For our last few months we rented a tiny but delightful flat in Duke Street, W1, opposite Selfridges. We knew that we would be very rushed to finish the Manoir in time for opening, and have little time to kit out the property, so we profited from our proximity to John Lewis, Marks and Spencer and Selfridges to buy practically everything we needed to furnish up our four self-contained apartments, three *chambres d'hôtes* and "restaurant" for up to sixteen. By the time the movers eventually came, in January 2004, you could only crawl round the little flat above Benjy's takeout, so buried was it under crates and boxes.

Looking out from the open barn towards the pebble "beach" around the swimming pool and the garden beyond.

By now it was clear that we were going to spend all the money we had, and more, on Raynaudes, and we could forget the idea of keeping a London bolt-hole to rent out and keep as a foot in the property market. Part of me was relieved.

And then there was the vexed question—when would we jump? The decision was to some extent made for us. Peter's job at AMP, in which he was part of a team setting up or buying financial services companies in other European countries, suddenly came to an end when the company changed direction.

We decided that we wanted our Raynaudes life to began just as soon as possible. We would finish the project in double quick time and open for business as soon as we could.

Those final months in London were action-packed. I was in my sixth year at *BBC Good Food* magazine, and, helped by the dream team of Mary Cadogan and Angela Nilsen in the Test Kitchen, it seemed the magazine could do no wrong. I finished my fifth year of writing a daily recipe for the *Daily Express* newspaper (with my mother as indefatigable recipe tester) and wrote my first full-scale cookbook, *The No-Cook Cookbook*, intended for urban cooks looking for a glamorous quick fix with minimum effort, which sold more than 30,000 copies. And at the BBC we launched a new food magazine, *Olive*. This was a project I had always wanted to get my teeth into, targeted at affluent professionals who love food, restaurants and travel.

At the same time as *Olive* appeared on the scene, another food magazine (*Delicious*) was launched headlong against *BBC Good Food*, which brought out all my competitive instincts. The previously serene world of food-magazine publishing suddenly began to look like *The Devil Wears Prada*, and I had to make special personal pleas to the magazine's old friends, such as Gordon Ramsay and Delia Smith, to stick with us. Fortunately, *Good Food* proved invincible.

When I broke the news of our French adventure to my magazine bosses, they were extraordinarily supportive, offering me a two-year contract as editorial director working across both magazines. I had always been convinced my then deputy Gillian Carter, with her cool intelligence,

would make a great editor, and she has taken the magazine from success to success—including the creation of the web site. And if there was a living embodiment of the *Olive* reader—bright, urbane and sparky—then that person is editor Christine Hayes. To this day I work with both magazines as a consultant, reviewing issues and discussing strategy.

It only adds to the delights of life at Raynaudes that ten minutes after serving a fabulous fresh breakfast on the terrace, complete with freshly baked croissants, fresh fruit salad, homemade yogurt, freshly squeezed

The terrace laid for breakfast.
The distinctive blue of the
shutters is the color of woad,
which used to be cultivated in
the region.

apple juice, raspberry muffins and four homemade jams, I can turn my attention to something even more serious—such as discussing what *BBC Good Food* and *Olive* can do next month to dazzle and bewitch its million avid readers.

So in January 2004, Peter and I took the plunge and moved full-time to a rather chilly Raynaudes, with four hectic months to go till the first guests arrived. As well as finishing a thousand small jobs, we also had to furnish and decorate the entire property. To the rescue came my friend from *Living* days Mary Carroll, at this time editor of *Homes and Antiques* magazine. When I told her confidentially about our plans for Raynaudes, she insisted on helping, and I do not know where we would have been without her. Everything that Ofir had brought to the architecture and design of the house, Mary brought to the decoration and furnishings. Many of the fabrics she chose were from Jane Churchill, supplemented by clever buys from Ikea (such as amazing pure linen for 3.50 euros a meter). From fairs and antique shops she also snapped up for us beautiful old linens to convert into cushions and throws, including an ornate, exquisite monogram of the letter Z that waited four years to come into its own.

When we were in our final frenzy trying to finish off the house, Mary arrived with her sewing machine and her friend interior designer Hilary Rudlesden. In ten days they hand-made 19 pairs of curtains, to say nothing of beautiful fabric bedhead covers, 24 cushions and even lacy cupboard fresheners. They softened and feminized the living rooms and bedrooms, and added subtle touches that suddenly made them look charming and very French.

They must also have spread the word that we were in dire straits, because other friends immediately headed out to help us. Jo painted about half a mile of skirting board—electrical whiz Kay wired up over thirty light fittings—Andrew chiseled into bare stone to get curtain rails horizontal—and Henrietta flew out to compile a booklet of touring information for foodie guests.

The orangerie faces on to the courtyard, providing a cool retreat among a collection of exotic plants from all over the world.

The markets of the Tarn and Aveyron are lined with stalls selling wonderful charcuterie, but we still find you cannot beat homemade. Peter is the terrine expert at Raynaudes, and this is his favorite, made either with or without the *foie gras*.

Duck terrine with foie gras and apricots

Serves 12

⅔ cup dried apricots, preferably organic unsulphured, halved

1¼ pounds duck breasts, skinned (or 1¼ pounds boned meat from a mixture of breast and legs, skinned)

2 tbsp Armagnac

1¼ pound pork fat (such as fatback, or if unavailable use fatty pork belly)

1 egg, beaten

½ tsp ground allspice

1½ tsp fresh thyme

1 tsp orange zest

8 large thin slices *jambon de pays* or other cured country ham, rind removed

¼ pound foie gras (*mi-cuit* or *bloc*) (optional)

Three hours before cooking, pour boiling water over the apricots to plump them. At the same time, take ¼ pound of the duck breast, cut into 6 long flat strips and marinate in the Armagnac.

When ready to cook, mince the remaining duck with the pork fat. Mix in the egg, allspice, thyme, orange zest and the Armagnac in which the duck strips have been marinating and season generously. If you wish, test for seasoning by frying a tiny nugget in a pan and tasting.

Line a terrine dish with the *jambon de pays*, leaving extra to fold over the top. Pile in half the mixture and lay on top the duck strips, the drained apricots and the *foie gras*, sliced into strips, trying to arrange them so that each slice you serve will feature all three. Finish enfolding with the *jambon*, put on the lid or wrap tightly with foil and bake in a roasting tin half filled with water for 90 minutes at 350°F (325°F convection). If you have a meat thermometer, the center should register 160°F. Leave to cool in the water, then chill for 1 to 3 days before serving.

MAKE IT LOOK GREAT

Though it is gilding the lily, we serve this on a bed of leaves, not too complicated a mixture, lightly dressed with a walnut oil vinaigrette and a few toasted walnuts. We serve another local delicacy as accompaniment— winter watermelon marmalade (*confiture de pastèque*).

We make this—as does every household in Raynaudes—
every November from the laboriously seeded and finely
diced flesh of *pastèque*, a hard-skinned, pale green melon
with whitish flesh harvested at pumpkin time. I add a
vanilla pod or two and the shredded zest of 2 oranges and
1 lemon to the marmalade when boiling with sugar, at the
ratio of 3 cups sugar to 2¼ pounds watermelon flesh.

RAYNAUDES SECRET

Lining the terrine: if you are
planning to unveil your terrine in
front of guests, by all means line
the ends as well as the sides
and top of the terrine with
jambon de pays to encase it
completely. If you are slicing it in
the kitchen, however, lining the
ends is a waste, as these end
slices are too tough and bacony
to serve.

The Bonnés

IF YOU DRIVE INTO THE HAMLET OF RAYNAUDES, the Bonnés' house is
the dove-gray villa before you turn past our lake. It was built in 1907,
and at the time was the epitome of refinement and elegance, with its
leisurely veranda—over which tumbles an ice-mauve *glycine* (wisteria)
—and pretty flower garden, filled with camellia and bluebells in spring,
followed by phlox, morning glory, begonias and geraniums of every hue.
Last year Mme Bonné—Mauricette—flaunted tradition. In her very front
and most sunny flower bed, where she normally tucks a row of leeks or
aubergines, she grew a bold stand of asters. "*Pour faire joli,*" she gave as
the reason. "*Pour les anglais!*"

Behind the villa is a 27-yard-long stone barn, used as a pigeon house
until a stoat got in last year and killed them all. It is also where M. Bonné
—Gilbert—overwinters his huge collection of lemon, orange and grapefruit
trees, abutilons, bottle brushes and oleanders—many now jungle size.

The road into Raynaudes runs past Mauricette's kitchen window, which
is always open, and if you listen as you pass you are quite likely to hear
accordion music. Sometimes it is Radio Cagnac, the local radio station,
sometimes a television concert—wide-smiled virtuosi with fingers
flashing over buttons and keys—but if you are lucky it is Gilbert himself.
He has three professional-quality accordions, one with his name picked
out in glittering mother-of-pearl.

Nearest neighbors M. and
Mme Bonné live life as they have
always done—cultivating their
fruit and vegetables and laying
up conserves for winter. Quinces
are a local delicacy.

The Bonnés do not miss much that passes in and out of Raynaudes, total population sixteen. Mme Dauzats, proprietor of a chain of local furniture shops, is a widow of some means and cuts a stylish dash when not on her travels round the world. Le Parc, her home across the road from the Bonnés, is the only house with an electric gate.

In the very rustic dwelling south of the Bonnés lives Mme Cayre. Georgette, also a widow, keeps a living larder of rabbits, hens and ducks, and every lunchtime at noon her son Jacques, now in his sixties, comes home for lunch. Until 2007 Georgette was the owner of a gray dog with a deceptive, crooked grin that was the bane of village life. In the last summer of its life it punctured a tire of the melon man's trailer with its bare teeth.

In the very center of the village is a beautiful, immaculately kept house so similar to ours that new arrivals for the Manoir often mistakenly knock at the Cluzels' door. There are in fact only three or four designs of house in the area, and we both happen to have the same one, athough as M. Cluzel has pointed out, his is 3 yards longer.

The Cluzels represent the Raynaudes Equator, that uncomfortable place where north meets south. Many years ago M. Cluzel, the most mild and charming of men, took a dislike to the village postbox which is set in the wall of his barn, and grew a thorny Queen Elizabeth rose over it. By the time the general fury over that died down (the rose is now rather pointedly trained to the right, like a Veronica Lake hairdo), the problem over the village bins had reared its ugly head.

South of the Cluzels live M. and Mme Regourd, the tidy and efficient local farmers who are to a large extent responsible for keeping Raynaudes as spruce and tidy as it is. M. Regourd is on the village council, and he thought the village bins, when their impending arrival was announced in 2003, should be positioned between the Manoir's front entrance, the Bonnés and Georgette. The north village—the Bonnés, Georgette and Mme Dauzats—violently protested, made threats regarding M. Regourd's three donkeys, and managed to get them re-sited 109 yards south.

Georgette (Mme Cayre) lives in the centre of the village. The dog in the picture is successor to the dreaded tire-puncturing beast.

Once a year, to thank the village for its cooperation and to apologize for the traffic and noise we bring into this rural hamlet (and indeed to do what we can to heal residual feelings over the dustbin debacle), we ask the whole village to lunch or dinner. The first time, we asked why no one minded the constant stream of hire cars, and people peering into their front gardens. "We love it," they replied. "You *animate* the village."

In the early days of the renovation project, Peter and I several times drove down from London, a trip of about thirteen hours door to door. Once we did it overnight, and arrived at Raynaudes in the morning. I will never forget the sight of Mauricette when she spotted our car come up the lane—she threw down her trowel and virtually pirouetted with delight.

This was followed by an immediate invitation to lunch, which was our first proper taste of French home cooking. The scene was Mauricette's kitchen-dining room, painted in shades of lime and jade, complete with two stoves, a period dishwasher, a dresser of favorite china, the television, and a round table to eat on. In traditional French households the lady of the house does all the paperwork and acts as social secretary, so to one side Mauricette also keeps a table and telephone for the purpose. Everything is always neat and tidy and clean and the meal arrives effortlessly, without fuss, bother or pretence.

And what a meal it is. We start with an aperitif—a dry white wine from the Languedoc—and cheesy biscuits. We drain the last drops of *apéro* in preparation for the red wine, a Bordeaux, because one glass will be used throughout the meal for wine, water—and more.

The entrée is a *terrine de canard*. Mauricette's terrines are coarsely textured, perfectly seasoned and taste richly of meat and herbs, accompanied by a wedge of the coarse, crusty, burnt-on-the-outside *pain au levain* (sourdough) that the bread lady from Le Ségur delivers to Raynaudes in her white van every Thursday and Sunday and calls *pain de miche*.

M. and Mme Cluzel. Like most of the villagers, Georges was born in Raynaudes and educated in the schoolhouse.

In this fertile part of France, there is such plenty in summer and autumn that even now country people are virtually self-sufficient. This is because they know the art of preserving everything—in duck fat (such as *confit* and terrines), vinegar or alcohol (cherries, raspberries, plums), or sugar (jams and preserves). Mushrooms, especially cèpes (or porcini), are cooked in oil, tomatoes are simmered into sauce, and both put in jars. To help them keep for months or even years, the jars are put into a huge boiler or sterilizer and simmered for an hour—a trick I now use myself with jam. Nowadays countrywomen like Mauricette have added another method to the list—freezing, which means they can enjoy luxuries such as asparagus all winter long.

The entrée is followed by a cheese soufflé, softly set and with a bright yellow color that denotes farmyard eggs. We are the only people in the village (apart from the Wealthy Widow) not to have a few chickens running round, though we have found a source of fresh farm eggs. In the next village, La Goussaudié, lives a farmer whose wife comes from the exotic island of Réunion in the Indian Ocean. I have befriended her to the extent that she will often sell me a couple of dozen eggs. Their young son Francis has taken over the running of the farm, and seems to have started a program of modernization. I hope this will not run to chopping down the enormous palm trees each side of the front door, which I guess, fancifully perhaps, provide Mme Mercadier with nostalgic memories of her tropical childhood.

Next is a guinea fowl, roast, cut into pieces and passed round to help ourselves, followed by a dish of stewed green beans. By British standards, vegetables are often drastically overcooked by the French, but eating the results, I can see why. Undercooked beans have a crunchy outside, a mealy center and a short-lived, grassy taste. Long braised they go silky, with a deep, rich, almost smoky flavor. The color is poor, nutritionally they may be compromised, but they are perfectly delicious, especially with a slick of olive oil and a few crisp pieces of bacon on top.

A cheese board is produced from nowhere, laden with three huge wedges of cheese: Cantal (from the Auvergne), Roquefort (from the Aveyron), and a piece of Brie, as a nod to the north. Gilbert eats cheese three times a day, starting with breakfast. His first drink of the day is a glass of rosé.

Next is invariably one of Mauricette's tarts: if you are very lucky, chocolate and walnut. This is so famed locally that when she contributes two or three tarts to the village dinner in neighboring Trévien on the feast of Saint Jean (June 24), they have to be closely guarded until dessert time.

At this point we finish what we are drinking and Mauricette produces a jar of her triumphant greengages in *poire Williams* liqueur (homemade, of course). Gilbert is a fanatic fruit grower—Mauricette says he has *"la maladie de greffer"* (grafting disease)—and so the road into Raynaudes is lined with apple, pear, cherry, quince and plum trees. The greengage goes into our wine glasses, with a hefty extra slurp of the *poire* liqueur, and we eat it greedily to make room for coffee. Which also goes into the same glass.

Georges Cluzel on his 1949 tractor in front of their house, built in identical design to the Manoir (but one bay longer).

As the meal has unfolded, Gilbert and Mauricette have been more and more enthusiastically chatting away, and Gilbert in particular has started to drift into *patois*, which in this area is a form of *occitane*. It is said that although there are hundreds of different forms of Occitan, a speaker from Menton can understand a speaker from Perpignan can understand a speaker from Biarritz.

M. Regourd and Sam off for a morning's hunting. The local woods teem with wild boar, deer, hare and pheasant.

At least in our area, however, *patois* has a slightly sad history. In the twentieth century it was heavily suppressed and school children were punished for speaking it. It was dirty and ignorant, something to be ashamed of. The first word of *patois* I identified was *allora* for *alors*, and when I asked Gilbert about it, he changed the subject. Just as he did the first time I mentioned the Maquis, or French Resistance—but about that, more later.

People assume that after three or four years in France you can speak the language fluently, but alas not so. Despite having had reasonable French before coming to live here, the more I learn, the more there is to learn. Whereas the English language consists of words that—like building blocks—you arrange in sequence to put across your meaning, almost every word in a French sentence seems to have a bearing on every other, a spider's web of agreements and conjugations.

Like so many things in France—indeed perhaps the language is where the problem starts—it is so *complicated*. Complication can be beautiful and fascinating—think of pâtisserie, jewelery, haute couture, fragrance, Impressionist painting, the music of Debussy and Ravel—but it can also be frustrating and time-consuming.

In September 2003 my linguistic shortcomings were brought home to me when France-3 asked if they could make a documentary about the Manoir, finishing with a cookery shoot broadcast live from their Toulouse studio. The film section at the Manoir went well, with the Bonnés in cameo role as adorable country grandparents and Monique unforgettable as funky *femme de ménage*, doing the rock'n'roll with her basket of cleaning products.

The studio session was when things started to go wrong. It was bad enough having to cook a three-course meal without a burner, oven or sink while talking about the history of willow pattern (about which I know nothing). During a particularly tricky piece of pastry folding, presenter Hélène Bassas asked me: "*Vous êtes là depuis combien de temps?*"

To which I replied: "*Une heure dix à peu près dans un four chaud.*"

(How long have you lived in France? An hour and ten minutes in a hot oven.)

Confit is the most delicious thing you can do with duck or guinea fowl. Developed over centuries as a way of conserving meat, you can eat this confit fresh, keep it for up to 10 days immersed in fat in the fridge or freeze it. Simply brown it before serving and you have a meal fit for a king.

Confit of guinea fowl

Serves 6 (easily doubled)

6 plump guinea fowl legs

3 or 4 cloves garlic

handful of thyme, roughly chopped

3 or 4 crumbled bay leaves

⅓ cup coarse salt

1 tbsp crushed black pepper

1⅔ pounds duck fat

Start a day ahead. Wash and dry the guinea fowl legs. Put in a large strong bag, preferably zip-lock, and use a garlic press to crush the garlic directly into the bag. Add the herbs and seasoning (not the fat), close the bag and use the bag to massage the flavorings evenly over the legs. Refrigerate in the bag overnight to cure.

Rinse the flavorings off the guinea fowl legs, dry and arrange closely in one layer in a roasting pan. Heat the fat until just about to boil and pour carefully over the legs (it is inclined to splash). You should have just enough to cover, but if your roasting pan is too big, you can turn the legs halfway through. Put in the oven at 275°F (250°F convection) for 1¼–2 hours. The legs are done when they are completely tender and slightly shrunk from the bone—do not continue beyond this or the meat will start to go stringy.

If keeping for a few days, you can leave the guinea fowl to cool in its "bath" of duck fat, then refrigerate. Otherwise, lift the legs on to plates to cool, taking care not to break them.

The fat can be reused three or four times. I find the best policy is to pour it when warm (but not hot) into large freezer bags, cool then freeze it. If you can freeze it in a flat shape (for example in a large zip-lock freezer bag) you can easily chip a lump off if you want a little duck fat for roasting potatoes, for instance. The dark brown "stock" that settles at the bottom of the fat should be discarded either before or after freezing as it is too salty to be useful.

To serve, bring the legs to room temperature. Heat a dry frying pan and add the legs, in batches if necessary. Check the skin is not sticking and periodically pour away the fat that exudes. The pan can splutter so have a spatter guard to hand. The legs take about 3–4 minutes per side to heat through and brown. I then slide them under a preheated broiler, skin-side up, for a really tasty crust.

Make it look great

The classic accompaniment to confit is sautéed potatoes or a ragoût of white beans, but at Raynaudes we break all rules and serve the confit on a bed of chervil risotto, or when chervil and parsley are in short supply, saffron risotto.

A final refinement of this dish (although not traditional) is to bone the confit—this is easiest done when the confit is still warm from its first cooking. The bone will slip out easily and the meat stay in a neat roll shape.

RAYNAUDES SECRET

Confit: although it seems laborious to cook the confit three times, the final broiling is what gives the skin a delicious, slightly charred, barbecuey finish. If you are making a cassoulet, or using confit as an ingredient in another dish, canned confit is very acceptable. If making it with duck, use four duck legs and cook for 2¼ hours. Guinea fowl and duck legs are usually sold with a small portion of the lower joint intact—what you might slightly gruesomely call the knee. Do not be tempted to trim this off before cooking as it will hold the skin in place and discourage it from pulling back and exposing the tender flesh.

The Garden

I NEVER WAKE UP ON A SUNNY DAY at Raynaudes without experiencing a small wrench. Am I in the kitchen this morning, or the garden?

For me gardening is a passion that satisfies absolutely and at every level. It awakens every sense. It is fulfilling in the short term—when you pick a sweet pea or tomato—and the long term—when you plant an umbrella pine. I only have to cross the little wooden bridge into the Manoir garden and I am in a world of choices: shall I do something physical (turning the compost heap or shoveling gravel), or fiddle about (taking a few cuttings, deadheading or snipping plants into a better shape)—or any of the dozen possibilities in between?

I even love the language of gardening, with its zany semi-latinization and volte-faces of nomenclature. Long before I had decided the location or design of the Manoir's cutting garden, to provide flowers for the house, I knew that it was going to contain an alphabet of flowers from amaranthus to zaluzianskya.

When we came to the Manoir there was no garden, or at least little we thought worth keeping. A witch-shaped conifer cast sinister shadows over one side of the house, and a columnar cypress hugged the east wall, like a pointed green chimney.

In every other way we were lucky. There were fine ancient pears and walnuts in the meadow and the lake was fringed with willows and poplars. By the front door was a mature catalpa, which casts welcome shade over the terrace. This had been one of a pair, and its fellow had

A corner of the herb garden, with French lavender (*Lavandula stoechas*), prostrate rosemary 'Pointe du Raz' and the white form of tender biennial *Geranium maderense*.

been struck by lightning (if in fact the pair was symmetrical, they were planted too close together in the first place). We learned this and other historical titbits thanks to the visit of Mme Alègre, who lived in the house during the 1960s. Several previous owners or inhabitants have at some point come and looked around the refurbished Manoir, invariably with amazement.

Then there was the oak copse, consisting of 100 young trees clustered around a natural pond. Over the following couple of years I was also to discover a thrilling wildflower population round the Manoir—dog violets, wild pulmonaria (*Pulmonaria saccharata*) plus, most exciting of all, thousands of wild orchids. So far we have found common orchid, lady orchid and tongue orchid, and last year I added a "rescue plant" (about to be asphalted into the road to Carmaux)—a monkey orchid.
In our first year the view across the orchid meadow to the Manoir was captured in all its jewel-like beauty by painter Libby Edmondson, prints of which sell prodigiously in the Manoir's little "shop."

Even when the orchids have come and gone, there are treats in store. The copse is lusciously carpeted with wild honeysuckle, and nightingales start to provide nightly entertainment, trilling away to the delight of guests dining on the Manoir terrace.

Between the house and the wood was a natural sheltered dip, facing due south. Standing here, with the hills rising in the distance and beyond them the Pyrenees, I thought, this is the place for the garden. It seemed rather stony, and the odd gnarled fruit tree showed someone had at some point taken an interest in the patch, but that was all I then knew.

What I had in mind was a square garden composed of smaller areas or "rooms." We got out our tape measures and hammered in sticks until we had a square of 36 yards. Back in London I spent evening after evening with graph paper, protractor and coloring crayons working on a design. The idea was to divide the garden up by means of paths and hedges in strict proportion to what I believed were our requirements: 40 percent vegetable garden; 20 percent fruit garden; 15 percent herb garden; 15 percent *jardin d'agrément* (pleasure or flower garden, for sitting in); 10 percent cutting garden.

I started by putting in two paths, one leading across the square directly from the house to the wood, and another diagonally across from one corner of the square to the swimming pool. I sketched in a lean-to greenhouse against the wall of the open barn (the hangar). Although there are precious few noncommercial greenhouses in the area, winter temperatures consistently fall to 23°F and I knew I would find it impossible to resist cultivating the odd curiosity. This is where I overwinter our brugmansia (datura) collection, which bring a glamorous touch of the tropics to the courtyard during the summer months.

Harvesting microsalads (radish, basil, coriander and rocket seedlings) for dinner.

The vegetable garden took the form of three triangular raised beds, marked by espalier apples and pears. The fruit garden, behind a hornbeam hedge, was a more conventional rectangle, with rows of raspberries, strawberries, currants, gooseberries, plum, quince, other speciality fruits and, subsequently, dessert grapes and myrtles. The herb garden was a small circle, with a sunny seat in which to sit and inhale the fragrance. The flower garden was divided into three, each with a theme: silver and scented plants, blue and white flowers, and winter.

As for the cutting garden, it was only in our second year here that I came up with a design I was happy with. Given that the Manoir garden is a sort of miniature country house garden, one day I realized it lacked one thing: a maze. So I devised a tiny maze of raised flower beds with wooden edgings. The rule for visitors is that if you want to get out, you are not allowed to step over a flower bed.

The whole garden was surrounded by a yew hedge, and all paths were gravel or bark. As we had always planned that Raynaudes could be run more or less by the two of us, it was vital that labor was kept to a minimum, so we found out where to buy vast expanses of plastic membrane to lay under gravel and bark and stop weeds. And no lawn—not anywhere.

The first winter we were aware that parts of the garden seemed very wet. I was not sure if we had accidentally punctured a stratum of subsoil, allowing an underground stream to find its way out, or perhaps there was always a *source* or spring on that spot. We should not really complain about the water at Raynaudes—it is sweet and soft (off the scale of softness, in fact, according to the testing kit that came with our dishwasher). But plants do not like to sit in soggy puddles and after a year or two it became clear many of the yews were suffering. We have had to patch in with hornbeam—a lighter effect that I am beginning actually to prefer to solid yew. We have also embellished the main cross path with a tunnel of wood and steel arches, designed by an ingenious local metal expert and clothed by yellow and white climbing old roses, many scented.

In front of the greenhouse is a collection of citrus. In a good year we have enough to make limoncello (page 204), marmalade and preserved lemons.

Once the garden was formed, it was time to start planting. During our last summer in London—the blazing summer of 2003—my parents had loyally babysat my plant collection in their Surrey garden, watering twice a day, and phoning when anything looked peaky. The full tally of 208 plants was loaded on to a trailer and driven down to Raynaudes by Peter that autumn. With a couple of exceptions (viburnum and rhododendron in 2004), it is legal to transport plants round Europe, and I prepared a full list of everything for Peter to show to customs. He was stopped at the barrier, and the official was amazed when he saw what was in the trailer. "I've heard of people taking the kitchen sink, but not the garden!"

It may seem puzzling that we chose to bring so many plants from Britain, when France has a thriving nursery industry of its own. But as a visit to any French garden center will show, the actual range of plants on offer—though often beautifully grown—is limited. Many of the rarities that now thrive here at the Manoir are virtually unknown in France: *Drimys winteri* (tall evergreen shrub with greeny-white winter flowers), *Berberidopsis corallina* ('coral plant', with dangly berrylike flowers), *Ehretia dicksonii* (actually a tree, but I pollard it to make vast rough leaves), *Lapageria rosea* (ironically named for the Empress Josephine, a twiner with fascinating waxlike flowers).

Guests sometimes ask me what my favorite plant is, and though I only grow plants I love (I give or throw away ones that I do not) the most impressive has to be *Magnolia* 'Nimbus', which we collected from Spinners, the New Forest nursery, a month before coming out to France. It grows against our most favorable wall. Throughout summer its colossal goblet flowers throw forth their all-penetrating lemon-vanilla scent: I swear you can smell it from the front door, 33 yards away.

Another favorite scented plant is *Cestrum nocturnum*, a tender member of the potato family with discreet greeny flowers known in the tropics as 'Galant de Nuit'. You would never give it a second glance until nightfall after a hot sunny day, when it fills the entire courtyard with a sweet, exotic fragrance.

Of course, for guests the main draw of the garden is not so much guess-the-smell games as the wonderful organic fruit, vegetables and herbs that it pours forth for use in the kitchen. After three years of trial and

error, I know what thrives in the garden and what it is better to buy at Carmaux market—though the widely varying rainfall makes each year different from the last.

Star of the Manoir vegetable show has to be tomatoes. When we first arrived at Raynaudes I noticed a pretty tomato plant growing wild in nooks and crannies around the property. I do not know if someone at some point dropped a tomato, or if it is a hybrid of tomatoes grown here in the past, but it is a distinctive plant, with finely cut leaves and a horizontal habit. Fruits are bright and zappy, and are best picked when the entire truss has ripened. We have naturally christened this 'La tomate sauvage de Raynaudes' and the seeds are for sale to guests.

When selecting vegetables to grow in the *potager*, I go for unusual and old-fashioned varieties you do not find in the local markets.

When she was shown the diminutive Raynaudes tomato, Monique, our dynamic *femme de ménage*, laughed. The following day she arrived with a tomato the size of a football, with bright red flesh and few seeds, grown by her boyfriend Yves. I kept some seeds and now grow this as 'Yves' Géant', though I have yet to compete with Yves' all-time best—a staggering 3½ pounds. Guests have sent me seeds from northern France and from the United States, bringing our tomato collection to about 20 varieties.

Other successes are zucchini—we grow half a dozen different varieties. Beetroot—purple, golden and striped. Carrots—all the colors we can lay our hands on. Sweet corn—because it is so difficult to buy fresh in France (the stuff you see in all the fields is strictly for cattle). Plus leaves galore, from spinach to dandelion to rocket to land cress. Because the summers are so hot, it is impossible to get salads established in the garden after May, so we resort to microsalads—radish, coriander, rocket, mustard and so on, sown thickly in trays in the greenhouse and harvested as seedlings.

Herbs are used copiously every night, and I soon realized I needed a herb bed somewhere else if I was to keep the herb garden looking decorative. As well as a huge amount of basil (which obligingly self-seeds), I have a flat-leafed rosemary with superb flavor sold to me (though I cannot find an official listing) as 'Spice Island'.

In 2005, our yearly lunch for the village fell on Saint George's Day, and we were able to take our drinks outside into the April sunshine. It was the first time the villagers had properly seen the garden, and I watched with delight as they tried to find their way out of the cutting garden maze, all moving determinedly in opposite directions and not daring to step over a flower bed.

M. Cluzel watched on amusedly. "Glad to see you have put back the garden," he said to me.

"What do you mean, put it back?"

It turns out that in all the thirteen acres at Raynaudes, we chose to put our "new" garden on the exact site of the Manoir's original, vanished *potager*.

If you have a walnut tree in your garden, make this aromatic liqueur, which has a fresh, almost menthol flavor. At our neighbors' house (for this is Mauricette's recipe) this is a joint effort—Gilbert picks and smashes the walnuts, Mauricette does the bottling.

Green walnut liqueur

Makes about 6½ cups

fresh, undamaged green walnuts to half fill a 8½-cup jar

about 6½ cups alcohol for bottling fruits, or vodka

about 2¼ pounds granulated sugar

You will need a wide-necked 8½-cup jar (which will be irreversibly stained by the walnut juice) and bottles for the liqueur (or use the bottles the alcohol came in)

Wash and pick over the walnuts, which should be green but firm. Bash each one once with a hammer so it releases its juices and put in the jar (this makes a lot of mess and the juice stains terribly). Half fill the jar with walnuts, then fill the jar to the top with the alcohol. Shake well and leave for three months.

Strain the green-brown liquid into a bowl or jug and discard the walnuts. Filter again through wet cheesecloth if you wish. Stir in 1⅓ pounds sugar per 4½ cups of liquid, dissolve, bottle and label. Store in a cool dark place for at least six months, but it continues to improve indefinitely.

MAKE IT LOOK GREAT

The liqueur is a gleaming dark brown color, and there is always a little sediment. We serve it in small glasses over ice.

RAYNAUDES SECRET

This recipe runs to a timetable. The walnuts should be picked—either off the ground, or from the tree—on the feast of Saint Jean, June 24. The mixture should be filtered and the sugar added in mid-September. You can start to drink the liqueur the following spring. Raw alcohol for bottling is available in all French supermarkets and wine shops. (If you cannot find it, use vodka.)

The Market

FOR MOST BRITISH PEOPLE WHO COME TO FRANCE, the first two lures
on the list are the weather and the food. And when you think of French
food, you think of the markets.

We are within reach of half a dozen, including the most popular in the
region, at St.-Antonin-Noble-Val. This is a market with bells on—organic
sourdough, handpicked grapes from Moissac, fig and cardamom jam
made by nuns, rare-breed meats. Our local market is more down to
earth, and it is where you will find me most Friday mornings. When we
made our program with France-3, the Carmaux market was one of the
most exciting segments. The highlight was an interview with the mayor,
in which he remembered as a child trailing round all morning behind
his mother, while she compared prices and observed the minutest
fluctuations. At the very last moment, she would pounce on the bargains,
four hours of diligence saving her a triumphant handful of *sous*.

In a countryside bristling with bastide villages and historic monuments,
Carmaux is notable for its extreme plainness. If Michelin maps had a
symbol for the opposite of "worth a detour", Carmaux would get it. But
I love it. An old mining town (for 400 years, until the 1980s) it is like a
wonderful British high street of the 1950s, even down to early closing
(Monday). You can find *everything* you need in Carmaux—stationery,
d-i-y, poodle parlour, picture framing, hairdresser, butcher, greengrocer,
chemist, gifts, printing, mobile telephones, signmaker, shoes, sheet
music, fashion, pâtisserie . . .

In the May and June of
2006 we picked 220 pounds of
cherries from our orchard to
make *eau de vie*.

When we arrived in the area, I could not work out why the name Carmaux somehow rang a bell. This nagged at me. One evening we had dinner with friends Peter and Bridget Dixon, who run a charming *salon de thé* in nearby Najac. We started to talk about the French Resistance, a subject best kept clear of among the locals, who regard it as a pretty sorry piece of history. Although there were some extraordinary examples of bravery among the members of the Maquis, of which the southwest was a stronghold, underground plotting and double-dealing provided irresistible opportunity to settle old vendettas and intrigues. "Lots of bodies down wells," remarked Peter. He found a book about the Resistance and copied some pages for me.

My grandfather, Jim Skardon, was a spycatcher. He started his career in the police and was transferred to MI5. (He is rather chillingly portrayed in Hugh Whitemore's play *A Pack of Lies*, which tells of a Ruislip household infiltrated in the early 1960s by MI5 to snare spy neighbors Peter and Helen Kroger.) His patient, gentlemanly manner concealed a ruthless interrogation technique and the cunning of a chess grand master. At the end of the war he was seconded to the Intelligence Corps and sent to Europe to round up traitors. Within weeks he helped bring in William Joyce (Lord Haw-Haw), but his most famous case was Klaus Fuchs, whose confession he extracted in 1949.

My grandfather was a fascinating storyteller. His favorites were his early murder cases as a detective, but he sometimes also talked about his adventures on the Continent from 1944 to 1946.

I settled down to translate what Peter Dixon had copied for me, and there I read about "*L'affaire Lord*". This was a complicated Fowles-esque case of double-crossing and infidelity, implicating alike French, British and German agents (in fact, it is impossible to know who was working for whom). Outcome? Murder—body down well. Scene: Carmaux and the surrounding hamlets. Who was sent by British Intelligence to investigate in 1944? My grandfather.

At the end of the war, my grandfather must have been driving around our very country lanes. I do not think they would have looked very different. I like to imagine he lit his pipe in the Café des Amis in rue Albert Thomas, probably against the backdrop of the same wallpaper that

is there now, listening for clues. He must have been the person who first told me about Carmaux, and he would certainly recognize the market, where I spend every Friday morning.

My shopping starts at Place Jean-Jaurès, where the small growers and producers (rather than *revendeurs*, or traders) set up their stands. I start with Yannick's fruit stall; although only in his twenties, he runs a fruit farm near Montauban producing strawberries, cherries, then apricots, then apples and pears and grapes, then kiwi fruits. I do a quick tour of the other growers—maybe picking up some leaves or mushrooms freshly gathered from the grower's garden or hedgerow.

The meadow is a haven for wild-flowers, including four varieties of orchid, watercress and local delicacy *repanchous* (black bryony—see page 68).

In March this is the place to head for two local specialities. *Repanchous* (or *respanchous*) is an extraordinary wild crop that looks like very fine asparagus and is pulled from local hedges and verges. Gilbert has shown me exactly where to find it in the Manoir hedges, and from March to late April you will see innumerable cars and vans parked up in country lanes as local people hunt for it. If you buy a bunch and do not wish to be marked out as a tourist, it is carried upside down (not like a bunch of flowers). After much research, I have established that the plant is black bryony. Be warned that everything about it, except the immature shoots, is poisonous, especially the luscious scarlet berries that you see hanging on trees like strings of beads in September. Its flavor is similar to asparagus but with a pleasantly bitter, beery aftertaste.

Following hot on the heels of *repanchous* are bunches of broccoli or cabbage tops, ideally picked just before the yellow flowers open. These are a delicacy served boiled *à la repanchou*, or simply as a warm salad tossed in vinaigrette.

In late summer/early autumn this corner of the market is also the place to come for cèpes, the wild mushrooms better known by the Italian name porcini. They grow in shady woodland and pop up a week or so after rainfall. Monique taught me how to prepare them. Brush off the dirt and trim away the inevitable bits damaged by slugs. Peel the base with a potato peeler and wash each mushroom quickly but carefully before drying on a rack (they stick to paper). Slice lengthwise about ⅓-inch thick, stems and all. Heat butter and olive oil (or duck fat if you have it) and fry the slices briskly with seasoning, not too many in the pan at once, until they start to turn a rich tan color. The heady aroma of sizzling cèpes is a cook's perk, almost as delicious as the actual eating.

When all your cèpes are fried, sprinkle with finely chopped garlic and plenty of chopped parsley, check seasoning and serve at once. When her boyfriend Yves has had a successful forage, Monique cooks cèpes in large batches and either puts them in jars of oil (then sterilizes them) or freezes them.

Our own organic lemons are soaked overnight to soften the zest, which is then macerated in alcohol to make limoncello (recipe on page 204).

Across the high street in the Place Gambetta is the main market. Manoir guests go wild for our cheese board, which Peter expertly introduces each evening (before dessert, in the French tradition), so this is my first priority. Hard-cheese lovers fall for Ossau-Irarty (Basque) or aged Comté. If you like strong soft-rinded cheeses, Maroilles from the north. If you like clean and creamy, Brillat-Savarin or Petit Robert. If you like blue, classic Roquefort or Fourme d'Ambert. If a guest declares he does not care for goat's cheese, Peter challenges them not to enjoy Selles-sur-Cher. Some of Peter's cheeses tell a story. The pyramidal cheeses of the Loire lost their tops when Napoleon cut them off with a sword. They reminded him of the Pyramids after his failed campaign in Egypt. Langres from Burgundy has a slight dip in the top which is by tradition filled with *marc de Bourgogne* or *eau de vie* and lit at table. Epoisses is the only cheese banned on French public transport.

The biggest crowds are in the rue Hôtel de Ville cut-through between Gambetta and the Place de la Libération. First stop here is M. Campos, who specializes in cornfed poultry and sells the finest pigeons in all France, from Mont Royal the other side of Albi. Mitou on the stand opposite offers a range of over 50 different sorts of olive, as well as every imaginable dried fruit and nut, and the local favorite, salt cod. In the Tarn salt cod is made into a sort of hot fish pie called *stoficado*. After Mitou you will find in quick succession the onion man, who sells everything from shallots to the *Appellation d'Origine Contrôlée* pink garlic from nearby Lautrec. The *aligot* man, recognizable by his Auvergne-style peaked hat, stirring a vast cauldron of deliciously gloopy cheese-and-*crème-fraîche*-enriched mashed potatoes. The spice lady, with every seed, grain and tisane you could ever imagine, including the most softly scented and flaky of cinnamon sticks from Sri Lanka. And Serge the mushroom man, with trays of fresh chestnuts, shiitake and oysters, plus huge white mushrooms "*pour farcir*" (to stuff).

And finally we are in the Place itself. I can rarely resist buying something from Sebastian the herb grower, who offers dozens of organically grown herbs and aromatics, from hyssop to mizuna,

The most famous local landmark is the fortified Cathar hilltop village of Cordes, a warren of medieval alleys and richly carved palaces.

horseradish to marsh mallow. But for me an even bigger draw is Alby
Foie Gras. Although I have always been vociferous in my objection to
industrially produced foie gras (at *BBC Good Food* we campaigned
against it), I have never believed that artisan-produced foie gras is a
particularly different "transaction" from any other sort of meat or poultry
farming. The southwest of France is the foie gras capital of the world,
and although it is so rich that not everyone acquires the taste, for many it
is the ultimate delicacy.

Foie gras comes in many forms. At the Manoir we serve it either hot,
sliced and quickly fried as an escalope, or in terrine form, the purest
being *mi-cuit de foie gras* (literally, half cooked). In late summer, I order a
special form of *mi-cuit* with a layer of fresh figs in the centre. For a very
short season from late November to January, goose foie gras is available,
at about double the price of the regular duck version. Just as the birds are
different, goose foie gras seems to me meatier, coarser, gamier than duck.

At the Manoir, the serving of foie gras is attended by a small ritual. Early
Victorian clergyman and satirist Sydney Smith said his idea of heaven
was "eating . . . *foie gras* to the sound of trumpets", and we like to give
Raynaudes guests a taste of what he meant. The most uplifting foie gras
accompaniments we have discovered are "And the trumpet shall sound"
from Part 3 of Handel's Messiah (sung by Bryn Terfel) and the Allegro
from Bach's Brandenburg Concert No. 2 (played by Maurice André).

Another Manoir dish gets its own special musical accompaniment.
One day at our local flour mill I met, by chance, a young woman who is
one of the few people alive to know the secret of making the genuine,
legendary *pastis du Quercy*. This is a sort of rum-scented apple tart of the
region (no relation to pastis the aniseed drink), made with an
extraordinary pastry which is stretched like a filo.

For special occasions I drive an hour to Michèle Cavaillé's workshop near
St Antonin to collect *pastis* to serve as dessert, the aroma of which almost
drives me to frenzy on the way home. The tart is such a work of beauty,
with its towering crumples of featherlight, snap-in-the-mouth pastry
dusted with icing sugar, that we dim the lights and put on Saint-Saëns'
swirling love music from *Samson et Dalila*, "Softly awakes my heart".
And it has to be sung by Callas.

This is an example of preserving at its most sophisticated—a sort of double preserve, as the prunes have already been gently dried for hours or days to transform them from plums.

Prunes in Armagnac

Makes about 36 prunes in Armagnac

1 pound prunes (unpitted)

pot of tea

½ cup granulated sugar

about 2⅛ cups Armagnac

You will need two 2-cup preserving jars

Our prunes invariably come from Agen, north of Toulouse, and we can buy them in many sizes and degrees of drying, including semidried. For this purpose I find large (*géant*), fully dried prunes are best. After steeping for a couple of weeks (they keep indefinitely), the prunes are lush and squelchy, good enough to eat on their own with *crème fraîche* to cut the sweetness or ice cream. They can be raised to divine heights in a frangipane tart (see page 84). Think we cut the frangipane tart?

When we run gastronomic weekends for guests I like to feature as many local delicacies as possible in the menus, so I process the pitted prunes and swirl them into just-churned vanilla ice cream before leaving to firm. Fabulous drizzled with a little of the Armagnac syrup.

To make sure the prunes swell, prick each one with a darning needle or sharp skewer in three or four places. Make a large pot of tea—any type except smoked—and when you have had a cup, and the tea is well brewed, pour over the prunes to cover. Leave overnight.

Put the sugar in a pan with ⅓ cup water, heat to dissolve and boil for a minute to make a syrup, then leave to cool. Drain the prunes and divide them between the jars, then add half the syrup to each jar. Now pour in Armagnac to cover the prunes, close the jar and shake to mix. Leave for at least two weeks or up to a year.

RAYNAUDES SECRET

Gleaming black prunes in thick syrup make a luxurious gift, preferably in a jar labeled with ideas for what to do with them. The darning needle tip is from Mme Bonné. When she demonstrated this to me in the summer of 2006, her right arm was broken (she had slipped and fallen in her courtyard) but, never daunted, she grasped the needle in the fingers sticking out of the end of the plaster and attacked each prune like a sort of jabbing machine.

Repanchous or *respanchous* are the young twining stems of the wild black bryony, collected from hedgerows in March and April. In other parts of southern France it is known as *tamis*.

Repanchous with quail's eggs

Serves 4

12 quail's eggs

1 bunch *repanchous*

½ cup cubed bacon

handful of toasted walnuts, chopped

fleur de sel (optional)

FOR THE VINAIGRETTE DRESSING

1 clove garlic, crushed

1 tbsp white wine vinegar

1 tsp Dijon mustard

2 tbsp olive oil

1 tbsp walnut oil

To make the standard Raynaudes vinaigrette dressing, whisk the garlic, vinegar and mustard till creamy. Add the oils and whisk again, and season.

Bring a pan of salted water to the boil, add the quail's eggs and simmer for 4 minutes. Drain, cool quickly in cold water, roll the eggs to break shells, then peel, starting at the blunt end. Halve 6 of the eggs, season all of them and set aside.

Plain white wine vinegar is almost impossible to find in France. Fortunately my friend Jeanne Strang, who wrote the best cookbook of the local cuisine, *Goose Fat and Garlic*, gave me some of her vinegar mother. This sinister gelatinous substance floats at the top of a *vinaigrier*, which in my case is a tall glass jar to which I add white wine. Over a month (three months in winter) it turns the wine to vinegar, which I then remove, bottle, keep for a month or two and use. Sometimes blackish, liverlike solids collect at the bottom of the *vinaigrier*. Although this substance is commonly thought to be the vinegar mother, it is not. It means you have in fact killed her (or drowned, as the French say) by adding too much wine, or letting her get too hot or cold, or starving her of air.

Wash the *repanchous* and trim off the bottom inch. Cut into 2–4 inch pieces. Bring a very large pan of water to the boil and salt generously—more than you would for other vegetables. Throw in the *repanchous* and cook for 3–5 minutes, till tender. Drain and leave in the colander.

Meanwhile, put the bacon into a dry frying pan and fry for 2–3 minutes until just starting to brown. Turn off the heat. Pour in the vinaigrette to warm, stirring all the time.

To serve, pile the *repanchous* into a large salad bowl. Lightly mix in the eggs. Pour over the warm dressing and walnuts and toss lightly. Taste a *repanchou*—it should be slightly bitter but, if too much so, sprinkle a little *fleur de sel* on to each serving. In any case, grind over black pepper.

MAKE IT LOOK GREAT

Fleur de sel is the "cream" of salt, snowy white and collected only from the top layers of sea salt. Ours comes from Noirmoutier on the Atlantic coast (where they also produce the finest of French new potatoes, apparently irrigated by sea water). We do not use it with abandon, but to add a discreet crunchy savoriness to mild-tasting dishes, or in this case, to mellow the *repanchou* flavor.

The Kitchen

HAVING WORKED FOR TWENTY-FIVE YEARS IN AN OFFICE, it is no surprise that my metamorphosis into chef has not been entirely smooth. I love it—after all, I spend my working life doing what other people do for pleasure during their precious weekends and holidays. But nothing prepared me for the stress and pressure of more or less single-handedly putting out a top-quality meal for up to twelve guests six nights a week, with a different menu every time.

To be fair, the difficulty is not just the cooking. There is so much to be done that I sometimes do not know where to start. What with gathering and preparing fresh produce from the garden, shopping, menu planning, cleaning up and cleaning down—plus, incidentally, the cooking—I work an eighteen-hour day seven days a week from May to the end of October.

Of course, part of the problem is that my enthusiasm runs away with me. If I were miraculously given an hour extra to spend on preparation this afternoon, I would be far more likely to whip up an iced sabayon sauce to accompany that cherry-almond tart rather than catch up on some sleep. The work seems to expand into all available space, and way beyond.

This tendency first became apparent as early as 1992, when I won through to the semi-final of BBC2's *Masterchef*, then presented by Loyd Grossman. Looking back, my menus seem fantastically complicated, as if to demonstrate just how much I could make in two and a half hours (bread, pastry, ice cream, fresh pasta, elaborate sauces . . .)

Behind the scenes, deputy cook Caro Garman. Each night's six-course set menu—from cocktail snack to after-dinner chocolates—is prepared from scratch.

So I try to keep things simple. One catalyst was the arrival of a friend who came to help for a couple of months in early summer 2006. After breakfast she would pop out to pick red currants and by lunchtime have them transformed into jars of gleaming, perfectly set jelly. Or I would ask her to prep up a raspberry and cinnamon torte and find it sitting in the larder finished and cooling. And she emptied the dishwasher! It was a reminder that in a kitchen one and one equals three.

Shortly afterwards we were joined by a remarkable young woman called Caro Garman, a professional food stylist whom destiny placed in a village a mere 2 miles away. She now cooks with me in the Manoir kitchen three mornings a week. And in the evenings, when we are more than ten at table, we are joined by Benoît, a student who earns holiday money waiting at table, while practicing his English.

If you have ever wondered what it is like to run your own professional kitchen like that at Raynaudes, here is a re-enactment of a day spent in it.

Cool, streamlined and not a millimeter wasted—the Manoir kitchen.

The scene is a small kitchen designed by Bulthaup, the German contemporary kitchen company. They worked within a space 20 yard square to create what Peter describes as a "lean fighting machine." In the middle is a small island with induction burner. A walk-in larder is packed floor to ceiling with ingredients. The rest of the equipment is largely what you would find in a normal kitchen (for instance, Neff double oven, American-style fridge) with four crucial exceptions: a Miele professional dishwashing machine, which dispatches the most groaning load in a mere 26 minutes. A Robot Coupe food processor (the Magimix having broken once too often). A Jura coffeemaker, which makes fiendishly strong espressos and cappuccinos, and even grinds the beans to do it. A gleaming stainless steel Musso ice-cream maker, which whips up the smoothest, whippiest ice creams and sorbets you ever tasted.

Wide drawers house a large collection of heavy-duty cookware, juicer and KitchenAid. A gadget drawer contains every imaginable slicer, peeler, scraper, cutter to speed up kitchen preparation. This is governed by two rules. One, if a gadget is not used in three months, out it goes. Two, nothing new can be put into it without something old being removed.

Not counting obvious things like knives (I use Henckel, Peter uses Japanese or ceramic), I have a few desert-island tools that I use every day.

1 Bench scraper. A 4x6-inch rectangle of stiff plastic that I use to handle and cut bread dough and clean the counter afterwards. Cost about a dollar.

2 Serrated peeler. For most peeling I use the cheapest, tinniest swivel peeler (actually rather hard to find nowadays), but my friend Sue gave me a new shark-shaped version with microscopic serrations, which even does the trick on tomatoes and peaches.

3 Masking tape. Because our kitchen is used by three people I insist everything is labeled. It is easy—scribble and stick. Also good for securing opened boxes of spillable foods such as rice.

4 Reusable nonstick silicone mat. I have cut out shapes to line all my baking sheets, tins and ramekins. There is even a thick black version to line the floor of the oven.

5 Two-inch paintbrush. If you are rolling out tricky pastries and bread doughs, especially when the weather is hot, you need to use plenty of flour. To prevent a floury finish, brush the excess off with a paintbrush before putting in pan.

6 Alligator chopper—you put an onion between its plastic jaws, press down and a steel mesh cuts it into tiny dice. Now joined by baby-Alligator for shallots and garlic.

7 Digital probe thermometer. Takes the guesswork out of baking and roasting. I use it to test when bread is cooked, to cook custard to the perfect point, to judge when roasts are done. If all my other gadgets were to be washed away, as Kirsty Young might threaten, this is the one I would wish to find on the beach.

The kitchen also has a total of eleven timers (five on the induction burner, two on the oven, three clockwork, one necklace-style in case I go into the garden), as the only way I can get through my timetable is to interweave different cooking operations. Sometimes different buzzers and bleepers go off at the same time, making weird duets and trios.

Although tiny, the kitchen can be organized into three work stations, one for me, one for Caro and one for Peter. It is a Manoir secret that Peter often contributes a course to the meal, his specialities being terrines and pâtés, and a range of tricky desserts.

8.10 a.m. Monique sets the breakfast table on the terrace while I get started on breakfast. I put the croissants in the oven (brilliant all-butter frozen ones from the posh frozen food chain Picard that are better than any I have found at a pâtisserie). Meanwhile I select the fruit for today's fresh fruit salad and peel, slice and segment it all. The salad is finished off with my magic ingredient, a slosh of cane sugar syrup. Then I either squeeze oranges, juice apples or rev up a smoothie in the blender.

Monique puts out the homemade granola and muesli, selects jams and jellies from our stash of homemade, places the homemade yogurts in a bowl of ice, pours a jug of iced water, takes out the fruit salad and juice and asks if there is anything else (I aim to produce some surprise most mornings, such as muffins, French toast or *madeleines*).

The Manoir is an especially magical place after dark—the night sky is so unpolluted it is an astronomer's dream.

9 a.m. The first guests arrive, and Peter takes orders for coffee or chocolate, which I make, or tea, which he makes. The chocolate is a new departure for us. Forget cocoa—you simply heat milk and a handful of 70 percent chocolate (we use Michel Cluizel), whisking constantly, till it almost boils. Peter spends the next hour looking after breakfast guests, who carry on arriving till 10 a.m., while I clear up after my fruit session and get down to work, unless it is a shopping day.

9.30 a.m. Caro arrives and we plan who will do what. I try very hard to stick to a rotation of five or six main courses, which makes life much easier, but the first courses and desserts change constantly, as do the appetizers, breads, salads and chocolates. We do our best to ensure guests do not eat the same thing twice during their stay.

The Manoir's flower garden, divided into silver, blue and winter "rooms."

If there are breakfast supplies to be made—cereal, yogurt, banana bread and so on—we start by making those. In high summer the garden is bursting with fruit. Caro or I will pick it, set aside what we need for cooking and make the rest into jam, or freeze them for smoothies. It is also a good time to get going on chocolates, which are fiddly and often need to be worked on in two or three stages as they cool. For some chocolates, such as florentines and *mendiants* (small discs covered with fruit and nuts) we need to temper the chocolate to make it shiny—an especially tricky process in hot weather.

I also like to get started on the day's bread. We make all the bread eaten at Raynaudes except croissants and brioche for toasting, and I have a repertoire of about twenty different sorts, which I make according to the menu, and what I fancy or have time for. By far the most involved is the sourdough. My culture contains wild yeasts collected at Raynaudes, supplemented by a culture sent to me from Vermont, which is reputed to contain yeasts from New England and Alaska. As sourdoughs go it is fast and furious, but the whole process takes two days. As for normal breads, I have found a way to fit them into my schedule better, by doing the second rise in the refrigerator—which retards it until I am ready to bake in late afternoon.

1 p.m. We are joined by Peter. There is only room for two stools in the kitchen, so if Caro is still here we take it in turns who stands up each day. I have a bottle of our local Cathar beer (the local mines may have been closed but we still have a fine brewery at Blaye-les-Mines), Peter has a glass of wine, Caro has a cup of tea. We eat cheese, or something left from last night. Before Caro leaves she prepares mirror-finish pots of butter for tonight's tables and chops any herbs for garnishing to dustlike fineness.

3 p.m. *The Archers* (France being an hour ahead). By now I aim to have the main course and dessert on track, and I check over the menu and finish off the details—tuile cookies to go with dessert, Armagnac truffles that are ready for dipping, miniature garlic soufflés to be prebaked as an appetizer, vinaigrette to be whisked and Roquefort sauce to be prepped ready to go.

To get our complex menus on to the table successfully takes considerable thought and organization, and I know exactly what can be done in advance and what has to be left to the last minute. It is not so much cooking ahead—which for me has connotations of dead-in-the-water reheated dishes—as breaking a dish down into its individual components and taking every stage as far as it can go.

For example, potatoes can be peeled in the morning, sliced two hours ahead, parboiled (if necessary) an hour ahead. Salads can be washed, dried and picked over in the morning, chilled, then tossed at the last minute. Dressings benefit from being made in the morning. Meat for roasting is best seasoned a day ahead, or failing that, in the morning, and is brought to room temperature before starting to cook. Stocks for sauces are best made in the morning, given an hour so the fat can be easily removed, reduced in the afternoon, finished at the last minute. Ice creams are best made and churned early in the day. Breads made with raising agents can be measured ahead, but need to be mixed and baked at the last minute.

4 p.m. Once or twice a week I make chicken stock, and once a week veal or beef stock. Though "invisible", these stocks determine what all our sauces, soups and risottos taste like. I do not make them for feel-good

Part-time waiter Benoît Vaysse charms Manoir guests, at the same time as perfecting his English.

reasons, to make me feel I am cooking with honesty and integrity. In fact, if I could find a powder, cube or canned product that tasted great I would probably never make stock again. In the meantime, I will carry on boiling. By mid-afternoon the stock is usually ready to be reduced and served either neat, as a jus, or with chilled butter whipped in at the last minute to add body and gloss.

6 p.m. If I am lucky I have half an hour in the garden, watering the greenhouse, picking last-minute herbs or soft fruits for dinner. I give Peter and Benoît a hand with the flowers for the table—with any luck, we can find something exquisite and dainty in the cutting garden, such as all-white sweet peas. If I have not managed it before, I print out our menu card. Until last year I used to write the menu on a blackboard, but as menus have become more ambitious and complex we have introduced a handsome card with our logo as watermark.

7 p.m. I shower and change into my dinner attire, which is jeans and a white T shirt, or on *dégustation* nights, a white short-sleeve chef's jacket. Benoît is amazed that my shirts and jackets stay white all evening. Many chefs seem to throw food around but I suspect they do not have to clean their own kitchens.

Peter checks his wine list. In four years he has made himself something of an expert on the wines of our local region, the Gaillac, which is the oldest in France (since Roman times) and one of the seven *Appellations Contrôlées* of the southwest. The wines are made from unusual grape varieties, including Braucol and Mauzac, and vary hugely in style (and quality). The Manoir's favourite wine producers are Michel Issaly at Domaine de la Ramaye and Christian Hollevoet of Domaine de la Chanade.

7.30 p.m. Peter puts on the music. We generally start with something classical—favorites are recordings of countertenor David Daniels, or Mozart piano concertos or the Sinfonia Concertante—before we move into some Latin (such as The Mambo Kings)—followed by Ella and Louis. We save Amália Rodriques for last thing at night. Peter serves the first round of aperitifs and offers the appetizer—which might be little mushroom tartlets, individual herb *clafoutis* or Roquefort shortbreads.

7.45 p.m. I make sure everything in the kitchen is under control, then join the aperitif party to spend ten minutes explaining the menu, how many different sorts of tomato there are in the salad, where the veal has come from, what Japanese wineberries are.

8 p.m. Dinner is served. On a normal evening, it consists of appetizer, entrée, salad or vegetable, main course, cheese, dessert, chocolates. A typical late spring line-up:

- appetizer of *carta di musica*—crackly paper-thin bread made on baking stones in the oven, served with a little dried fig and a slug of rum tapenade in the style of Marseilles

- entrée of a softly set Roquefort and chive tart, with olive and rosemary bread

- salad of wild watercress (from the stream that runs through the meadow), dandelion and toasted walnuts

- roast fillet of Ségala veal (the Ségala is an area covering part of the Tarn and Aveyron, famous for its free-to-roam, humanely raised veal and beef) with Armagnac jus and large fat potato wedges cooked in goose fat

- cheese (Peter's domain, consisting of up to half a dozen cheeses in a state of perfect maturity), served with homemade quince paste

- Coupe Raynaudes (a luscious combo of caramel and chocolate ice creams, chocolate sauce, praline, cocoa nib tuile)

- coffee and fresh passionfruit truffles

On *dégustation* evenings, we serve appetizer, amuse-bouche, entrée, fish or vegetable course, main course, cheese, dessert, chocolates. A typical midsummer menu:

- appetizer of tiny soufflés of pink Lautrec garlic

- shot glass of Roquefort foam with mini Roquefort *croque-monsieur*

- entrée of sole in a fresh horseradish sauce, with soft dinner rolls

- boned quail with fresh cherries, smashed potatoes

- cheese

- strawberry napoleon (layers of thin shortbread, homemade mascarpone and garden strawberries, drizzled with coulis)

- coffee and mini chocolate macaroons

Apart from dishes that are already on the go (such as a roast) or the occasional dish that takes longer than others, I tackle the menu course by course. Peter and I synchronize constantly to try and make timings smooth and perfect. In early summer we keep things moving, because it may get chilly, and in late summer the same, because it will certainly start to get dark before the meal is finished.

My 1892 Blüthner piano, which was almost written off by the plumber.

We do not have a chance to sit down during the meal and eat ourselves, but if there is enough we do have something as we go along. Any scraps from plates are put in a bag for Benoît's dog, Napoli.

I am sometimes asked if things ever go wrong, and although not every element of every meal is just the way I want it, things largely go as planned. The worst evenings have been caused by circumstances beyond our control. For twenty-four hours in September 2006 the mains water was cut off, and because we were constantly told it was about to be reconnected, we did not cancel dinner. Friends in neighboring villages arrived with every bottle they could find filled with water, and we boiled water from the swimming pool to wash up.

In summer we are near enough to the Pyrenees to catch the edge of the odd storm, and when the electricity flickers I rush to turn every appliance on full, in the mad hope that if the power fails I can cook the whole meal on residual heat.

10.30 p.m. Peter collects the order for coffee or tea. Peter makes the teas, I make the coffees. I cannot work in a kitchen with pots and pans piling up—I need to feel things are under control—so I clear up as I go along, but at this point Benoît takes over, cleaning any outstanding pans, filling, emptying and running the dishwasher.

Peter and I head out to chat with guests. Some evenings, I am asked to lull guests with a little piano music, which I hope is as delightful and relaxing for them as it is for me. One of the drawbacks of being in the kitchen all evening is that I am in a bit of a vacuum socially—beyond names I know next to nothing about our guests, so this is a chance to rectify it. Peter is very discreet and non-gossipy, and we do not spend time talking about people behind their backs. And obviously we never talk about guests to other guests.

Midnight Benoît goes home. Peter and I head for the office, he to record meal details on guest accounts, make up bills for tomorrow morning and deal with reservations received during the day, me to plan menus and keep on top of food ordering and shopping lists.

St-Juéry is a town on the outskirts of Albi, the capital of the Tarn, where our neighbors, the Bonnés, have a cozy winter home. It is also said to be the origin of this ritzy steak dish.

Steak St-Juéry

Serves 6

FOR THE SAUCE

3½ tbsp unsalted butter, softened, plus 2 tsp extra

3 tbsp Roquefort cheese

1 shallot, chopped finely

3 tbsp Marsala or port

⅔ cup beef or chicken stock

2 tbsp *crème fraîche*

FOR THE STEAKS

6 fillet steaks

a little olive oil and butter

handful of chopped toasted walnuts, flaked almonds and pine nuts

chopped parsley

Mash the butter and cheese till smooth or, if you prefer, put in a small plastic bag and knead together through the plastic. Shape or press into 4 or 5 pieces, and refrigerate.

In the remaining butter in a small pan, fry the shallots for 3–4 minutes till transparent but not brown. Add the Marsala and reduce to a syrup, then the stock and reduce again to a syrupy consistency—it should be about 3 tbsp, bubbling with small tight bubbles. Set aside, still in the pan, and cover.

Season the steaks and fry for about 3 minutes per side in the oil and butter.

Set aside to rest while you finish the sauce by bringing the reduced juices to the boil, then lowering the heat so the sauce stays warm but does not boil. Whisk in the butter-cheese mixture piece by piece to make a thickish, glossy sauce. Whisk in the *crème fraîche*.

Slice each steak on the diagonal into 3 thick slices and pour over the sauce. Sprinkle with the nuts and parsley and serve at once.

RAYNAUDES SECRET

The rich and silky sauce, which is prepared ahead and finished in moments before serving, is also excellent with chicken or a roasted fillet of beef. For the beef, I rub a 2½-pound tenderloin all over with a little oil and seasoning (plenty of coarsely ground black pepper). Roast at 450°F (400°F convection) for 20–30 minutes, depending on how well you like it done. I aim for the center to read 125°F on a meat thermometer.

The dessert that won my *Masterchef* quarter-final. The figs need to be made at least a day or two ahead so they become syrupy. The recipe is also exquisite with prunes soaked in Armagnac (you will need about 20, pitted) or peeled, cored, halved or quartered just-ripe pears (you will need about 4—serve this version warm, unglazed).

Fig frangipane tart

Serves 8

FOR THE FIGS

10 figs

syrup made with 2½ cups water boiled with 1 cup sugar for 5 minutes

FOR THE PASTRY

1⅛ cups all-purpose flour

1 tbsp coarse or medium semolina

8 tbsp cold unsalted butter, cubed

4½ tbsp confectioners sugar

2 egg yolks

FOR THE FRANGIPANE

1 cup blanched almonds (or ground almonds)

1 stick (8 tbsp) unsalted butter, room temperature

⅓ cup plus 2 tbsp superfine sugar

1 egg

Blanch the figs in boiling water for 3 minutes, drain, put in jars and cover with hot syrup. Can be made a month ahead.

For the pastry, whiz the flour, semolina (which adds slight extra crunch) and butter in the processor, then add the sugar and egg yolks till the mixture comes together. Form into a cylinder and chill or freeze till solid (if intending to grate by processor in the next stage, shape so cylinder fits down feed tube). Coarsely grate by processor or hand into the tart pan, spread over the base and up the sides, then firmly press into position all over. Scrunch up a large sheet of baking paper (easier than foil and sticks less), lay over pastry and up sides, add baking beans and bake at 375°F (350°F convection) for 20–25 minutes until firm and pale golden all over, carefully removing paper and beans after 15 minutes. Turn the oven down to 300°F (275°F convection).

Meanwhile process the whole almonds (if using) till powdery, then add remaining frangipane ingredients and mix to a sticky consistency.

Trim away the tough stalk top from the drained figs. Halve and put cut-side down over the pastry in one layer. (Depending on size you may not need them all.) Spoon the frangipane mixture to cover the figs and tart base, without overfilling (if you have excess frangipane, you can top up the tart after it has been in oven for 10–15 minutes). Bake for 1 hour to 70 minutes, till golden and set (check the frangipane is no longer sticky using a skewer).

RAYNAUDES SECRET

When baking blind, rich pastry tends to slump at the edges, however much trouble you take with prechilling, paper and baking beans. If necessary, after removing paper and beans, while the pastry is set but still soft, use a spoon to gently push the sides back up into position.

FOR THE GLAZE (optional)

2 cups syrup from the figs

juice of ½ lemon

ROSE-SCENTED CREAM

⅔ cup heavy cream

2 tsp granulated sugar

2 tsp *eau de vie de prunes* or other fruit brandy

1 tsp each of rose water and orange flower water

You will need a deep 10-inch tart pan.

Delicious warm, but can be glazed if serving cold. Boil the syrup till thickened and syrupy, add lemon juice and brush over the tart. Just before serving, whip the cream and sugar until starting to stiffen, then add the liqueur and flower waters and whip till stiff. Serve separately.

MAKE IT LOOK GREAT

This is a beautiful gleaming tart, so put it on a large plate and slice in front of guests.

Coming of Age

WHEN IN 2002 WE FIRST STARTED TO DREAM about living and working in France, we had a concept firmly in mind. We would set up a comfortable, unpretentious *maison d'hôtes* with wonderful fresh food. And in a beautiful, fascinating part of the country—as far south as possible.

For the record, the location is spot-on. A short—ravishing—drive in any direction will take you to fairy-tale hilltop villages, such as Najac, or the plunging gorges of the Aveyron. If you want picturesque, there is Albi, with its momentous fortified cathedral (the biggest brick building in the northern hemisphere). If you are into art, we can offer Toulouse-Lautrec in Albi, Goya in Castres. If you fancy modern, how about Norman Foster's viaduct at Millau, currently the highest in the world, plus the caves of Roquefort as an (ancient) sidetrip?

The climate is pretty well perfect, too. Summers are usually long, dry and sunny, and the sky a remarkable cerulean blue. The other seasons are strongly demarcated. Autumn is gloriously fine and colorful, and winters cold and very wet (down to 23°F for a week at a time). The most remarkable difference from the British climate, however, is that any fine day between November and April it can become shirts-off weather. We have eaten lunch on the terrace on New Year's Day and sunbathed in March.

So much for the setting. As for the accommodation, we did not at that time have any sort of pretensions that we might be opening any sort of hotel. We had in mind something more modest, a simple *maison d'hôtes* with gîtes attached.

Monique Suarez, our trusty *femme de ménage*, has been with us from the start.

Maison d'hôtes means literally "guest house," or b&b. (The French word *hôte* means rather confusingly both "host" and "guest.") *Table d'hôtes* means that the hosts offer dinner (in theory hosts and guests eat the same meal round the same table). A *gîte* is a farm building converted for holiday self-catering use. In practice the quality of gîtes varies drastically, and those sleeping vast numbers are especially to be avoided—unless you are happy sleeping in the bed great-grandma died in, and putting babies to bed under the stairs. So slender is the connection to our sleek ultramodern duplex gîtes that soon after arriving at the Manoir we rechristened ours apartments.

At Raynaudes we are approaching the maximum number of *chambres d'hôtes* and apartments the Tarn allows before you are classified as a hotel and run into problems with fire escapes and bar licenses—four *chambres d'hôtes* and three apartments. All are incidentally named after the ladies of the village—Mauricette, Ginette, Angèle (Gilbert's late mother) and Georgette—and families who have played an important part in Manoir history: Bonné, Caillol, Montfort.

We had hoped that by keeping things simple and modest, we would be able to enjoy a better, healthier, more relaxing lifestyle than the London ratrace. From the start, the division of labor came very naturally. I am happiest doing physical work such as cooking and gardening. I also love ironing, so I did that for the first two years until Monique (who also loves it) proves she is infinitely better at it than I. I also mastermind what would in corporate life be called "communications"—printing, marketing, PR. And I also provide the stock for the Raynaudes "shop," in a corner of the salon.

Peter excels at more cerebral jobs, plus anything requiring patience and application—reservations, finance, guest accounts, housekeeping and maintenance. From the very first arrival we realized Peter was also far better than me at "front of house"—meeting guests, advising them on touring, suggesting places for lunch, serving at dinner. He is also much more interested than I am in wine, and in cheese.

Guest rooms Mauricette (with paintings by Peter's father) and Ginette (with paintings by Manoir guest Libby Edmondson).

From our first season, however, bookings started to flow in, and we soon forgot any thoughts of relaxation. Before leaving London I had assiduously contacted all my friends in the magazine business, hoping they might at some point give us a mention. *Homes and Gardens* was the first to feature us, followed swiftly by the *Saturday Telegraph Magazine*, *Financial Times* and *Country Living*. An American guest wrote to *Travel and Leisure* in the United States about us, then we were picked up by *Condé Nast Travele*r U.S.

Napoli the Flying Spitz.
Thanks to Benoît, our waiter and Napoli's owner, he enjoys regular scraps of *foie gras* and fillet steak.

As the first year rolled by, we found ourselves mentioned in French magazines too—*Elle* and news magazine *L'Express*. And before we knew it, we were turning up in guidebooks—Travel and Leisure's *The World's Best 500 Hotels* and boutique-hotel bible *Mr and Mrs Smith*. We are now well into our second scrapbook of press cuttings, the result of which is a tally of over 1,100 visitors in our first three years. Even more gratifying is that in our fourth year at least half our visitors are returning for the second or third time.

Obviously Peter and I could never keep up with this level of business without help, and we have gradually built up a small team. It all started with Monique, who was a tip-off from the Wealthy Widow. Monique appears to run on a different voltage from mere mortals. This former rock'n'roll champion, widowed in her forties, sleeps only four hours a night. Before coming to work she waters her psychedelic garden and calls in on her aged mother to make breakfast and set up lunch.

Her morning at Raynaudes will see her mopping floors, ironing a pile of six king-size sheets, four tablecloths and sixteen napkins on the Miele rotary iron, polishing windows with her adored micro-fiber cloth and arranging a small vase of flowers for the downstairs lavatory. As she departs she briefs Dani (assistant housekeeper, whose shift begins as Monique finishes) on refreshing *chambres d'hôtes* Ginette and Angèle, cleaning the orangerie *à fond* (i.e. deep cleaning), and sweeping out the open barn.

Monique is a treasure trove of lore and true insight passed down through generations. She loves all food, and knows how to cook everything. She loves all flowers and knows how to grow everything. And it will come as no surprise that she adores all colors. On a Monday she might arrive in a turquoise jumpsuit teamed with sandals with big pink roses on top. Another day, lime-green striped harem pants with a yellow floral blouse and green earrings. Mme Bonné saw her in the supermarket one day in top-to-toe white—she looked "like a pearl."

However diligent and motivated it may be, labor in France does not come cheap, and for this and other reasons, our original aim of pricing rooms and meals at the Manoir modestly has gone out of the window. Early guests politely suggested that we were undercharging, but now we have entered the category of "reassuringly expensive."

Take the *chambres d'hôtes*. When we first raised prices, we thought it was time to put a small innocuous vase of flowers in each room. At the next increase we added toweling robes and slippers, then bath sheets, then bowls of fruit. Breakfast has gone the same way: what started as a bowl of muesli, bought yogurt, a croissant and fruit juice has turned into a ravishing array of treats and surprises, different each morning and requiring the utmost skill to plan, assemble and prepare.

The list of extra services we introduced in 2007 included a choice of aperitifs, Wi-Fi system (and computer in case you did not bring your own) and "shop" (two cabinets of exclusive Manoir souvenirs). Ask ahead and you can book bicycles, massage and beauty treatments, guided walks, chauffeur-driven tours. We have almost inadvertently turned a modest b&b into a select boutique hotel.

Running the albeit small team at Raynaudes has in itself created a mountain of extra administration and expense. Peter could write his own book on filling out employment forms, tax declarations and social charges, but, in a nutshell, for every 10 euros we pay one of our employees, we pay an extra 8 euros to the French state. (Incidentally, the employee pays about 4 of his or hers to the French state too.)

We do, of course, see the benefits of high taxation—the best roads and health system in Europe, to start with. On the other hand (though we never expected it to) our life here is never going to make us rich.

It is a good thing that Raynaudes brings so many rewards in other ways. The guests, for a start. When friends beg us for horror stories about guests from hell, we are sorry but we have to disappoint them. No one has ever stolen a picture, torn pages out of books, dug up a rare plant, broken a lavatory, shouted at another guest, fallen asleep in their soup, come in late drunk, gone away without paying . . . On the contrary, 50 percent of our guests actually write us a thank you note when they get home. And because I keep a log of every menu we have ever served to every guest, I can look back over it to jog all sorts of memories, happy or hilarious, of our wonderful guests. Raynaudes also seems to spring to guests' minds when they are thinking about special occasions. Just one example: in summer 2006, at the end of a romantic holiday here, French-American Marc Choaniere asked Adney Bowker for permission

to marry his daughter Hallie. Marc and Hallie returned from Seattle to celebrate their wedding with thirty-five friends in March 2007. Hallie, a designer, created the most romantic of events, a dream of blossom, lace and fairy lights. Locals said the tent could be seen from Canitrot (only 2 miles away, but still deemed remarkable).

As well as the decoration and the bride's film-star beauty, highlights for Peter and me were local traiteur Henri Vidal roasting a pair of suckling pigs on an open fire outside the tent. And the local taxi service bringing vast ice-encrusted platters of *fruits de mer* from our Albi fishmonger—by ambulance, with the blue light flashing. Last but not least, Hallie's sister-in-law Amanda has the initial Z in her name—so after four long years that monogrammed cushion came into its own.

The surrounding landscape and hamlet of Camalières (above and overleaf), separated from Raynaudes by just two fields.

THE RECIPES

Appetizers

Cocktail CLAFOUTIS

Parmesan, nigella *and* sesame BITES

Roquefort *and* walnut SHORTBREADS

Mushroom *and* onion marmalade TARTLETS

FOAM of Roquefort

Herb OMELETTES stuffed *with* ricotta

FRITTATA of leeks *and* ham

"LE CAKE" aux olives *et* reblochon

Sardinian sheet music BREAD

TAPENADE in the style of Marseilles

LIQUEUR *de* cassis

Beginning well is critical, and at Raynaudes our aim is to produce exciting, tasty, beguiling morsels to whet the appetite, without filling guests up so they have not got room for chocolates.

Cocktail clafoutis

Makes 24

3 tbsp plus 1 tsp cornstarch

1 cup milk

2 large eggs plus 2 egg yolks

1 cup heavy cream

½ tsp salt

pinch of cayenne pepper

TO FLAVOR

grated cheese, plus halved olives, diamonds of red pepper, prawns, fried bacon, fried mushrooms or chopped herbs

You will need two 12-cup mini-muffin trays (or, if you have only one, to bake batches in succession)—silicone is ideal

Clafoutis is a very popular dish in the area, a softly set batter pudding studded (usually) with cherries or pears or plums, and presented as a family dessert with dollops of *crème fraîche*. This is a savory modern take on this old favorite.

Put the cornstarch in a bowl and whisk in half the milk till smooth, then the eggs and yolks, the rest of the milk, the cream and seasoning. Spoon 2 tbsp of the mixture into mini-muffin molds and bake at 400°F (375°F convection) for 15–18 minutes, topping each clafoutis with a little cheese plus one of the other suggested toppings halfway through. Leave to cool in the tin till just cool enough to handle, then remove with a spatula or table knife. Serve at once, but do warn your guests the centers may still be hot.

You can make the clafoutis several hours in advance, or even freeze them. Reheat in a hot oven for 5–10 minutes before serving.

Guests arrive at Raynaudes at all hours, but very often the first thing they would like is a chilled glass of the local Gaillac wine. We keep a supply of these savory bites always on hand to accompany drinks.

Parmesan, nigella and sesame bites

Makes about 50

2⅔ cups flour

3 cups Parmesan, grated

2½ sticks (20 tbsp) unsalted butter

½ tsp cayenne pepper

1½ tsp fine sea salt

1 tsp coarsely ground black pepper

2 tbsp sesame seeds

2 tbsp nigella seeds

Put everything except the seeds into the processor and whiz until the mixture is well mixed. Add the seeds and continue processing until the dough comes together, like pastry.

Form into three or four cylinders—about 1–1½ in diameter—and wrap in plastic wrap. Chill for at least 4 hours, till firm.

Cut into ¼-inch slices, space ½–¾ inches apart on baking sheets and bake at 350°F (325°F convection) for about 17–20 minutes, till nicely golden—do not undercook. They keep perfectly for a couple of weeks in an airtight container.

Our most elegant appetizer—crisp, light and delectable. Once baked, you can keep the shortbreads for a week or so in an airtight container. Sandwich them up to two hours before serving.

Roquefort and walnut Shortbreads

Makes 40–50 filled shortbreads—allow 2 or 3 per guest

1¼ cups all-purpose flour

pinch of cayenne

½ cup Roquefort cheese

1 stick (8 tbsp) cold unsalted butter, cut in pieces

1 egg yolk, plus a little beaten egg to glaze

40–50 walnut halves

FOR THE FILLING

small Boursin cheese flavored with pepper, or ¼ cup mascarpone blended with 3 tbsp Roquefort and ground black pepper

Put the flour and cayenne in the processor and whiz to mix. Note that you do not need to add salt to this dough on account of the cheese. Add the Roquefort and butter and whiz to crumbs, then the egg yolk. The mixture needs to be fairly homogenous or the shortbreads will be dangerously flaky when baked, so if necessary scrape down the sides of the processor with a spatula and whiz again.

Lay two pieces of plastic wrap on the work surface and turn out half the dough on to each. Fold each up in the plastic wrap and shape into a flat disc about ¾-inch thick. Chill for at least a couple of hours, or overnight is better —if it seems too hard to roll out when you start it will become amenable in a matter of minutes.

Roll out on a well-floured surface to ¹⁄₁₂-inch thick and cut into 1–1¼-inch coins—I have a fluted cutter for the purpose. Use a spatula if necessary to transfer to a nonstick baking sheet, or one lined with a nonstick silicone mat.

Press a perfect walnut half lightly but securely on to half of the shortbreads. Glaze shortbread and nut with a little beaten egg, trying to avoid run-off on to the baking sheet. Leave the other half plain. Bake for 12–15 minutes at 350°F (same for convection) until nicely golden. Allow to cool.

To fill the shortbreads, set out the bases in a row and the walnut tops in another row. Roll small balls of the filling between your palms and gently press on to the bases. If the filling is too sticky, use a teaspoon instead. Lay the walnut shortbreads on top and lightly press on the walnut to stick the sandwiches together. Transfer to a serving plate.

We have been serving this at Raynaudes since the day we opened, and hardly a guest leaves without asking for the recipe. Those not in on the secret marvel at the crispness of the "pastry".

Mushroom and onion marmalade tartlets

Makes 12

1 tbsp olive oil and 1 tbsp butter

1 onion, chopped

1 tbsp granulated sugar

½ pound mushrooms, sliced

thyme or rosemary leaves, finely chopped

12 medium slices of *pain de mie*, or white bread

butter, at room temperature, for spreading

grated Comté or Cantal (or Cheddar) to sprinkle on top

You will need a 2¾–3-inch diameter glass or biscuit cutter and a tartlet pan, preferably nonstick

Heat the oil and butter and fry the onion for about 7 minutes till softened and lightly golden. Sprinkle with sugar and seasoning, then add mushrooms and thyme or rosemary and cook over a high heat until the mushrooms are done, about 5 minutes.

Cut out circles of bread. Lightly butter one side of the bread, then put butter-side down in the pan and press into place. Put the mushroom mixture on top and sprinkle all over with cheese. Bake at 425°F (400°F convection) for about 10–15 minutes until golden. Serve hot.

MAKE IT LOOK GREAT

From making these many times, we have discovered that if you are quite generous with sprinkling the cheese, some tends to land on the area of the pan between the tarts. This bakes to a lacy crispness. If you are a neat sort of person you may wish to snap or trim it off but resist— it is almost the best bit.

When we first started serving foams at Raynaudes, guests were mystified—they had not come across such a thing. Then Heston Blumenthal demonstrated them on television and the craze swept the nation.

Foam of Roquefort

Serves 6–8

⅔ cup Roquefort

⅔ cup milk

1 tbsp olive oil

¾ cup *crème fraîche*

You will need an ISI Gourmet Whip soda siphon, or other make, plus two N2O capsules (see overleaf)

If the fad has passed you by, foams are featherlight mousses made by aerating a liquid of creamy consistency with nitrous oxide (N2O) in a soda siphon. Foams are light and whippy and are invariably served in very small quantities—such as in shot glasses. You can also make hot foams, foam sauces and dessert foams, and indeed in many modern French restaurants you will eat all these in the same meal.

Foams appear on our menus about once a week, as a whimsical pre-first course to sharpen the appetite. Translating for French visitors I looked up foam and found the word *écume*—but be warned, this means scum.

In a blender process the cheese, milk and olive oil. Add the *crème fraîche* and buzz briefly. Put through a sieve into a large jug, forcing any remaining bits of cheese through with a spoon. Whisk again and pour into the siphon.

Shake the siphon and screw in one capsule of N2O then another. Leave for at least an hour. Shake well. Fill shot glasses and serve immediately.

MAKE IT LOOK GREAT

Depending on the firmness of your foam, you can suspend a tiny cube of Roquefort on top and/or dust with paprika.

Make Your Own Foams

FOAMS—*espumas* in Spanish—were made famous by Spanish superchef Ferran Adrià at his restaurant El Bulli near Barcelona. Although he did not invent them, he started making them out of extraordinary ingredients, from sea urchins to bubblegum. I tease guests at Raynaudes that when a chef has mastered foams he moves on to vapors and inhalations. If you come back next year, I say, dinner will be good for the waistline but horrifying expensive. And invisible.

If you are the sort of person who is frightened of a pressure cooker, foams are not for you, as the technology—gas capsules and whooshing sounds—is initially alarming. But foams make a fun and quirky addition to one's repertoire. Even today there is a shortage of published information, so you need to be prepared to learn as you go along.

Siphons come in 500ml and 1-liter sizes. In my view, 500ml is ample for nonprofessional use, as it will produce at least 20 foams in one go. The manual that comes with the machine should have information to get you started, but here is what I have learnt by trial and error, and some troubleshooting tips. *Important note*—make sure you buy N2O capsules (labeled for cream or chantilly) and not CO2 (soda)—which will work but make the foam taste fizzy.

MIXING YOUR FOAM

Foams need to be assertively flavored and seasoned otherwise they taste of air. My most successful flavors have been Roquefort, smoked salmon, sorrel and petits pois, all made by blending the main ingredients (cooked, in the case of sorrel and peas) with cream and putting through a fine sieve. The consistency after blending and sieving should be like cream. One strong flavor works better than mixing more than one.

Season generously to taste, using salt, pepper, lemon juice, pinch of sugar, Tabasco, cayenne. A drop of alcohol—for instance, brandy for Roquefort, Pernod for pea—can heighten the flavor. Remember that the seasoning will be dulled both by chilling and the aerating process. And when seasoning, do not add coarsely ground pepper after putting through the sieve, as it can cause clogs.

For a less creamy, more moussey foam, you can reduce the amount of cream and add gelatine. For gazpacho foam, for instance, I make a simple gazpacho, blend and put through a fine sieve into a container. To 1 cup of gazpacho, I whisk in a scant ½ cup cream and two gelatine leaves that I have soaked in cold water, drained in my hand and dissolved in the microwave in a few tbsp gazpacho. Having made these additions it is worth putting the mixture through the sieve one more time.

FILLING THE SIPHON

The rules are—shake and shake again. After filling the siphon, screwing on the top and ensuring the valve is in the right position (this varies from model to model), shake the siphon vigorously to coat the interior of the device with the mixture.

Next screw in the gas capsules. On my (1 liter) siphon you can use two or three—I have only ever needed two.

I am not sure why, but however much trouble I take to ensure my valve is correctly shut, it can happen that the gas starts hissing as soon as I start to screw in the first capsule. The solution I have found (by trial and error) is to continue to shake while I am screwing in the capsule (not the easiest operation), and, if that does not work, quickly turn the siphon upside down, which seems to set the valve up properly. After that, the second capsule normally behaves perfectly.

CHILLING THE FOAM

We only serve chilled foams at Raynaudes, although warm foams and superfluffed hot sauces are possible. I make them in the morning or the day before to give them time to set.

Shake the apparatus once or twice while the mixture is cooling in the fridge—if it contains gelatine, this stops the mixture settling in a solid lump at the bottom of the siphon. I shake again before and in between serving the foams into glasses, to distribute the mixture round the inside of the siphon. Even so, you must expect to waste a lot, as you will find when you unscrew the siphon for cleaning.

DISPENSING FOAMS

Aim to make them small and cute, to eat with a teaspoon. We always serve them in shot glasses, either long or short.

Dispense a try-out foam just before serving to check texture. If it is very soft you may have to hurry the foams to the table the moment they are in the glasses. Usually the texture is firm enough to support a little piece of Roquefort,

a tiny diamond of smoked salmon, or a few cooked peas, to point up the flavor as well as make it look pretty.

One of the harder things about serving foams is that you cannot see inside the siphon to know how much mixture you have left—you have to guess. Rather than run out with two shot glasses to go, I tend to fill all the glasses three-quarters full, then go back and top them up.

If despite your endeavors you run out of foam, here is an emergency procedure that might save the day. Warm the siphon under lukewarm running water to mobilize the contents (in case they have set at the bottom of the canister) and try again. If by this time you can hear there is liquid in the canister, but you have used up all the gas trying to dispense it, you may need to screw in a new gas capsule.

SERVING FOAMS

We always serve foams with a crunchy accompaniment. At its most simple, this might be fennel seed bread sticks (put a well-floured portion of basic bread dough after proving through the tagliatelle attachment of a pasta machine, brush with beaten egg and dot with fennel seeds before baking at 350°F (325°F convection) for 20–25 minutes). Or a miniature tart shell filled with scrambled eggs (on which we put a few cooked peas or a little smoked salmon) or *pipérade*, made by frying shallots, garlic and red pepper and stirring this into scrambled eggs. Or, for the last word in luxury, Roquefort and walnut shortbreads (see page 103).

Thin delicate omelettes are left to cool, then rolled up around a ricotta filling and sliced in the style of sushi. Tasty, elegant and all ready in advance—just what an appetizer should be.

Herb omelettes stuffed with ricotta

Serves 6–8

FOR THE FILLING

handful of basil and parsley, roughly chopped

1 cup ricotta

3 tbsp grated Parmesan

FOR THE OMELETTES

1 clove garlic

handful of chives, chopped

4 eggs

3 tbsp grated Parmesan

a little oil, for frying

Make the filling first by whizzing the ingredients in the processor. Check seasoning—it should be good and tasty. Scrape into a bowl.

Put the omelette mixture into the processor bowl (no need to wash it up) and process.

Heat the oil in a medium frying pan and when hot pour in one-third of the omelette mixture. When it has set, slide on to a board. Repeat to make 3 omelettes.

When cold, spread the ricotta on the top of each omelette (use it all) and roll them up neatly. Set aside on a board till ready to serve.

Slice each omelette on the diagonal into 6 or 8 pieces.

Abundantly strewn with fresh herbs, a frittata makes a generous snack to serve with drinks: I am no purist and I like to stack it up with tons of flavor. Allowed to cool and wrapped in foil, it is also the best picnic dish.

Frittata of leeks and ham

Serves 6–8

3 tbsp olive oil

½ pound new potatoes, scrubbed, dried and thinly sliced lengthwise

1 tbsp butter

1 leek, cleaned and thinly sliced

2 slices ham, cut into thin strips

FOR THE EGGS

8 eggs

½ cup heavy cream

1 tbsp flour

1½ cups grated cheese, plus extra for sprinkling

1 tsp salt

2 tsp mustard

splash of Tabasco

freshly chopped thyme, rosemary, chives or parsley, plus extra for garnishing

You will need a 12-inch frying pan that will fit in the oven

Heat half the oil in the pan and fry the potatoes, turning often, for about 15 minutes, until golden and tender. If you prefer, you can do this in a small roasting dish in the oven heated to 400°F (350°F convection) for 30 minutes.

Remove the potatoes from the pan. Add a splash more oil and the butter and cook the leek, seasoning lightly, for about 5 minutes. Add the ham and cook for 2 minutes longer. Leave for a moment to cool.

Mix all the remaining ingredients together in a large bowl and taste for seasoning. Now stir in the leek and ham mixture.

Heat the remaining oil in the pan and pour in the egg mixture. After a minute or two, use a spatula to allow uncooked egg to flow beneath the cooked layer. Once the frittata is starting to firm up, scatter the potatoes over. Cover and cook for about 5 minutes, moderating the heat to avoid burning (your nose will tell you).

Transfer to the oven, scatter with a little extra cheese and bake at 375°F (350°F convection) for 7–10 minutes till golden and just set.

MAKE IT LOOK GREAT

Leave the frittata to cool in the pan for a few minutes, then slide it out on to a board. Strew with the herbs reserved for garnish, and cut into squares or rectangles, rather than wedges, which are too big and difficult to balance when you are trying to hold a drink and a conversation at the same time.

Using Fresh Herbs

Almost every savory dish served at Raynaudes is lifted by the addition of fresh herbs. By this I do not mean mere decoration—I don't add whole leaves or sprigs—but chopped or sliced, to brighten flavor and add impact.

Different herbs need to be treated differently. Parsley is best extremely finely chopped—practically to dust. To achieve this, the parsley must be bone-dry, stems carefully removed (for the stockpot) and your knife freshly sharpened. Chopped parsley keeps for a good 48 hours in the fridge. I administer it (and its more aniseedy cousin chervil) very generously.

Chives, tarragon and coriander (cilantro) do not need to be so finely chopped, but only do this an hour or two ahead or they dry up. The smaller stems of coriander are packed with flavor and do not need to be removed.

The woody herbs—sage, thyme and rosemary—need to have leaves carefully removed from stems, then finely chopped.

Basil is treated differently from the others, and leaves are best roughly torn (at the last minute) or piled and rolled (like cigars) to be thinly sliced into a chiffonade—again at the last minute. The only time I chop them is when incorporating into a sauce or stuffing that will not be cooked.

I find the best treatment for mint is to pick small leaves and keep them whole, though I rarely use mint in savory dishes.

Although full of flavor, herbs are accommodating and, with the possible exception of mint, it is hard to add too much. Herbs lead the eye, so put them at the focus of the dish—for instance, on the meat rather than on the vegetable.

In the past three years French cooks have been swept by a craze for "les cakes." I am not sure how the misunderstanding occurred, but by cake they do not mean something round and sweet, but something loaf-shaped and (usually) savory.

'Le cake' aux olives et au reblochon

Makes 3 loaves, each serving 6

(1 loaf for now; 2 for the freezer)

1 cup cubed pancetta

handful of black olives, rinsed, dried, pitted and coarsely chopped

generous ¼ cup Parmesan cheese, coarsely grated

4 cups all-purpose flour

1 tbsp baking powder

¼ tsp cayenne pepper

1 tsp salt and plenty of ground black pepper

1 cup cubed Reblochon or other semisoft cheese

2 tbsp freshly chopped herbs

1 cup milk

3½ tbsp melted butter

1 large egg

¼ cup *crème fraîche*

We serve the Raynaudes "cake" in slices with aperitifs—it is especially elegant when baked in a dainty cocktail size. I managed to persuade a local catering supplier to stock small foil loaf pans—this recipe makes enough for 3—or you can make one big loaf in a 5x9-inch loaf pan. You can vary the flavoring as you choose—fried mushrooms, diced ham, herbs or other tasty morsels.

Fry the pancetta till just beginning to go brown. Leave to cool and mix in the olives.

Grease the pan or pans and sprinkle half the Parmesan evenly over the base. Whisk the flour, baking powder and seasoning in a large bowl (easier than sifting). Mix in the Reblochon, herbs, pancetta and olives.

In a small bowl, whisk the milk, butter, egg and *crème fraîche*. Using a large rubber spatula, fold the wet into the dry until just mixed—the mixture is meant to be thick and sticky—and stop when it is just combined. Turn into the pan or pans, sprinkle with remaining Parmesan and bake for 30 minutes (small pans) or 45–50 minutes (large pan) at 350°F (325°F convection), till a skewer comes out clean, though be aware that if it hits some oozy cheese it will come out sticky regardless. Cool in the pan for 10–15 minutes then turn out and serve warm.

This is a very unusual bread taking the form of a thin, crisp sheet—hence the name, *carta di musica*. If you imagine thin melba toast, you get the idea.

Sardinian sheet-music bread

Makes 4 large sheets

⅔ cup warm water

2 tsp fresh yeast (if using dried, see page 220)

2 cups bread flour

1 tsp salt

1 tsp olive oil

You will need a baking stone (see below)

If you are interested in bread making, this is great fun to make in the kitchen, and the sheets—which buckle when you toast them—look very dramatic in a tall pile served with evening drinks. There is another bonus: if there are any left over, they makes the most remarkable crunchy sandwiches.

Start the dough by mixing the water and yeast. Put the flour, salt and olive oil into your food processor and whiz, then add the yeast mixture. Process till the mixture comes together and then count to 45. Turn out and knead briefly on the work surface, then divide into 2 balls. Put in lightly greased bowls and leave in a warm place to prove until doubled in size. Heat the oven with the baking stone to 475°F (450°F convection)—this can take 30–40 minutes.

When ready to bake, turn the first ball onto a lightly floured surface. Trying not to create folds or creases in the bread, roll out to a large rectangle about ⅛–¼-inch thick. It is more important to get the bread thinly rolled out than to make a good shape. To get the dough into the oven, improvise a baker's peel by sliding a rimless baking sheet under the dough, then slide it on to the baking stone.

Watch through the oven door. After a minute or two, the dough should puff amazingly either into a football, or else a very puffy flatbread. Get ready to remove the bread. You want to catch it before it is brown or crusted, so count to 30 and then remove using the baking sheet as before.

RAYNAUDES SECRET

Baking tiles are very useful, even more so than pizza stones. There is no mystique about these—they are simply tiles laid on your oven shelf. We made our own from two leftover terra-cotta floor tiles. One is 12x12-inches, the other Peter cut to 4x12-inches, and I put them side by side to cover an entire oven shelf (with a little space all round to allow air flow). I am told the thicker the tiles the better. You need to allow ample preheating when using baking stones or tiles. My tiles are used regularly, not just for *carta di musica*, but also when I am making rustic loaves.

When the bread is cool enough to touch, use scissors to cut round the edge and peel the bread apart to make two thin sheets. If the dough did not puff very well—and sometimes it does not—you will need to saw the stuck bits apart with a knife. This will make no difference to the finished result. Check the inside of each sheet and rub or scrape any excess dough away with your fingers or a teaspoon.

Repeat with the other piece of dough. You will have 4 thin sheets of *carta di musica*.

While you have the oven hot, toast each of the sheets on each side– you may be able to fit two at a time—until crisp and brown in patches. You can retoast before serving if you think it needs it, but the bread should stay crisp in a sealed bag or box for a day or two.

Make it look great

To serve, we drizzle the sheets with extra virgin olive oil and grind over coarse salt. Guests snap off a section and crunch it. The crumbs go everywhere, so I only make this on a fine day when we are eating outside. This advice is especially pertinent if you decide to serve it with a dip, as we often do, because the bread is so brittle.

If you have never made your own tapenade, you will not know what you are missing. This is our favorite tapenade formula, but you can easily to customize it to your own taste.

Tapenade in the style of Marseilles

Serves 4–6

1 clove garlic

1 dried fig, trimmed and cut into quarters

1 tsp capers

2–3 anchovies, rinsed, filleted if necessary

1 cup black olives such as Kalamata, rinsed and pitted

chopped parsley

squeeze of lemon

Process the first four ingredients till finely chopped, scraping down sides of the processor occasionally. Add the olives, parsley and lemon juice and process again, till as finely chopped as you wish. The tapenade should be moist rather than sloppy, and somewhere between smooth and chunky.

Adjust balance of flavors to taste. If you like it harder-hitting, add more garlic, anchovy and caper. If you like it lighter and fresher, more lemon and parsley. You can add a little heat with cayenne pepper or *piment d'Espelette*. You can also make it with green olives.

I learned the trick of adding rum from Thane Prince at the Aldeburgh Cookery School—it is not so odd as tapenade is a speciality of France's Mediterranean ports, where a keg must always have been to hand. Start with ½ tsp and add more if you enjoy the punch.

MAKE IT LOOK GREAT

Several years ago I went on a touring holiday in Syria, and marveled at how beautifully the cooks served the various dips that are a feature of Middle Eastern cuisine. They presented them in wide shallow dishes, drizzled generously with oil and dotted sparingly with seeds—such as cumin—or herbs, usually in a simple geometrical pattern. As well as pleasing on the eye, this is practical, as a shallow dish makes it easier to scoop the dip up with *carta di musica* or crudités.

This homemade liqueur has a beautiful ruby-raspberry color and a slightly viscous consistency, and is stronger than most store-bought cassis. With wine or champagne, as a kir or kir royale, it makes an elegant aperitif.

Liqueur De cassis

Makes 2–3 litres

2¼ pounds black currants

4¼ cups good quality red wine

about 3⅓ pounds sugar

about 3⅛ cups Armagnac or cognac

You will need screw-top bottles (better than corked because the liqueur is sticky and corks get messy)

Wash the fruit and pick it over, removing as many of the stems as you have the patience for. (The fruits on the Manoir black currant bushes ripen in succession, which means that we can just about keep up with the arduous job of picking them, which is during our peak season for guests. You can freeze the currants at this point, and make the cassis when you have time.) Dry in a colander, then put in a large bowl with the wine and leave to macerate for 48 hours.

Whiz in batches in a food processor and tip into a jelly bag or muslin. Leave to drip and then squeeze the bag to get through as much juice as possible. Put into a preserving pan with 5 cups sugar for every 4¼ cups of juice. Note the height of the liquid in the pan by dipping in the handle of a wooden spoon and measuring the depth.

Stir over moderate heat till the sugar is dissolved, then regulate the heat so the temperature stays above blood heat but well below simmering. Check temperature every half hour or so. After 2 hours the mixture will be slightly syrupy, and the liquid level will have reduced slightly (check with the spoon). Leave to cool.

When cold, add the Armagnac: one part Armagnac to three parts of black currant.

First Courses

Escalope of *foie gras* on brioche *with* grapes

Robert's Roquefort *and* chive TART

Salade aveyronnaise

Slow-roasted tomatoes

Twice-baked garlic SOUFFLÉS

Deconstructed RATATOUILLE

Roulade of Roquefort

Seared sea scallop on boudin noir *with* parsley sauce

Fennel SOUP *with* goat's cheese

Fillet of Dover sole *in* horseradish sauce

Lemongrass-coconut SOUP

Foie gras means simply fattened liver. In our region it can come from duck (year-round) or goose (short season at the end of the year). It is so rich that in escalope form it needs only short cooking over high heat.

Escalope of foie gras on brioche with grapes

Serves 8 as a starter

1 fresh foie gras (*foie gras cru*), about ⅔ pound

a small bunch of white grapes

FOR THE BRIOCHE

2 eggs

¼ cup milk

2 tbsp Grand Marnier

2 tsp granulated sugar

2 tbsp unsalted butter

8 ½-inch-thick slices of brioche

a few chopped chives and fleur de sel, to finish

RAYNAUDES SECRET

Beef Rossini: sometimes at Raynaudes we serve an updated version of this old-fashioned classic of a steak topped with foie gras and truffles. Ours consists of roast fillet of beef with wild mushroom sauce, with an escalope of foie gras on brioche to accompany. To make this, follow the instructions above, omitting the grapes and chives and substituting Armagnac for the Grand Marnier. Cut the brioche slices into 2¾-inch circles using a round cutter.

I have long been an opponent of industrial foie gras, usually from Eastern Europe, but having visited farms in southwest France and read up on the subject, I believe eating artisan-produced foie gras is no crueler than eating other poultry or meat. I would much rather be re-born as a duck for fattening than, say, a chicken (even free-range). Our foie gras comes exclusively from Alby Foie Gras (see page 246).

Slice the foie gras crosswise into 8 slices of equal thickness. Season on both sides with salt, pepper, a dusting of confectioners' sugar and flour, put on a plate or board and refrigerate.

Halve and seed the grapes.

Mix the eggs, milk, Grand Marnier and sugar with a good pinch of salt and set aside.

When ready to cook, get all ingredients out. Set the oven to warm and put in it a baking sheet, a small ovenproof dish or bowl and 8 serving plates—not too large, as this is a small, rich dish. Heat half the butter in a large frying pan. When it is sizzling, dip the bread briefly in the egg dip and fry for about a minute on each side, till brown. Transfer to baking sheet and put in the oven to keep warm.

Add the remaining butter and, when sizzling, add the grapes, Stir them about for about 3–4 minutes over a high heat, seasoning well, then transfer to the ovenproof dish and keep warm.

Wipe out the pan and heat over high till smoking. Add the escalopes and set the timer for 1 minute, then flip them and cook the other side. (Check before each minute is up—the escalopes need to be richly browned with tiny charred bits, but not actually burnt. If they are cooking too fast, flip them before time and turn down the heat slightly.)

During the second minute, get the warm plates out, put a piece of brioche on each one, surround with a few of the hot grapes and top the brioche with foie gras. Sprinkle with chives and a little *fleur de sel* to add a salty crunch, before serving immediately.

When we were creating the Manoir, I asked my friend Robert Carrier, then living reclusively in Provence, for advice. He gave me many inspiring suggestions for dishes, including this superb, featherlight Roquefort tart.

Robert's Roquefort and chive tart

Serves 6 or 8 as a starter

1¼ cups all-purpose flour: replace 1–2 tbsp with semolina or cornmeal for crunch

salt, pepper, pinch of cayenne

6 tbsp unsalted butter

FOR THE FILLING

good handful of chives and parsley, roughly chopped (save a pinch of chives for garnishing)

generous cup mascarpone

7 tbsp Roquefort

1 tbsp unsalted butter, softened

3 eggs

generous cup *crème fraîche*

You will need a 9-inch tart pan, about 1¼-inches deep

Make the pastry by processing the dry ingredients, adding the butter then just enough water—2–3 tbsp—so the pastry just begins to form a ball. If possible chill for an hour, then roll out thinly and line the pan. Again if convenient, chill or briefly freeze the pastry case. Crumple up a big sheet of parchment paper then uncrumple it and lay it over the pastry. Cover with dried beans and bake at 375°F (350°F convection) for 20 minutes till firm. Remove paper and beans and continue baking for 5 minutes till the base is dry but not cracked.

Make the filling by whizzing herbs, mascarpone, Roquefort and butter in the processor till smooth. Add the eggs, process well, then the cream and seasoning: pepper and a pinch of cayenne (no salt). Pour into the hot pastry case and immediately put in the oven, still at 375°F (350°F convection) for 25 minutes, till golden, slightly puffed and just set in the center. Serve at room temperature.

RAYNAUDES SECRET

Savory tarts: three important tips. Don't throw away excess pastry after rolling out—scraps can be useful to patch cracks that appear towards the end of blind baking. Make sure the blind-baked pastry case is piping hot when you pour in the filling so that if the filling does find a hole it is instantly sealed. And if you appear to have too much filling, discard rather than overfill.

This salad is on the menu at every restaurant for miles around Raynaudes, and with good reason. Our version is not the simplest and by no means the most economical, but I believe it is the best.

Salade aveyronnaise

Serves 6 as a first course (4 as a main course)

1⅛ pounds cherry tomatoes, halved

1 clove garlic

5 tbsp walnuts

3 large handfuls of baby spinach or other mild salad leaves

large handful of basil leaves

2½ cups cubed bacon

7 tbsp Roquefort, cut into chunks with a small sharp knife

FOR THE DRESSING

2 tbsp sherry vinegar

4 tbsp olive oil

Put the tomatoes in a small roasting pan and crush the garlic directly over them using a garlic crusher. Drizzle with a little olive oil and season, then roast for about 15 minutes at 375°F (350°F convection), until slightly shriveled. Turn the oven down and toast the walnuts in another pan for about 15 minutes, till fragrant. Chop them roughly. You can do the tomatoes and nuts ahead if you wish, but if so, warm them before composing the salad.

Toss the spinach and basil (leaving the leaves whole). Season lightly.

Heat a frying pan and gently sizzle the bacon for 3–4 minutes till lightly browned. Keep warm.

Allow the pan to cool. Stir the dressing ingredients together and pour into the pan. Bring to a boil, stirring (the vinegar will smell strong), then pour over the salad and toss to wilt slightly. Add remaining ingredients, holding back a few crumbs of Roquefort and some of the best-looking walnut pieces. Toss and transfer to plates, decorate with the Roquefort and nuts and serve warm.

MAKE IT LOOK GREAT

After trying every implement, and combination of implements, in my kitchen drawer, I have concluded that the only way to present a salad attractively on the plate, at the same time ensuring that it is perfectly dressed and all the components are correctly distributed, is to use your hands.

Slow-roasted tomatoes

During August and September the tomatoes are literally dropping off the bushes at the Manoir, and I am always looking for recipes that use them in large quantities. This is my idea of coping with the glut: the tomatoes are swiftly prepared, roasted in the oven then either made into a soup, or frozen for the winter. The tomatoes are so good you can use them as they are in salads (they are like squelchy sun-dried tomatoes, with a sweet flavor)—for instance, Salade aveyronnaise, in which you can use them to replace the more quickly roasted cherry tomatoes.

Take large, ripe, well-flavored tomatoes. Wash them and halve them across their equator. Take a large roasting pan and pour in a thin layer of olive oil, then put in the tomatoes, quite closely packed but in one layer. Peel some garlic and cut it into slivers, then poke a sliver in each tomato. Or you can chop or crush the garlic and sprinkle over. Strew with salt and pepper and a dusting of sugar.

Roast for about 2 hours at 350°F (325°F convection), till shrunk and beginning to singe at the edges. Leave to cool.

At this point you can pass the tomatoes through a food mill for a roasted tomato soup. This is good served hot or cold, with a lemon cream made by mixing *crème fraîche* with seasoning, a little lemon zest and lemon oil.

The tomatoes keep for a week in the fridge, or you can freeze them. I find the best way to do this is to open-freeze them, then pack into freezer bags.

Raynaudes is not far from the garlic capital of the southwest, at Lautrec, south of Albi. Lautrec garlic is a special variety, protected by an *appellation d'origine contrôlée*, with pink skin. It keeps well and the cloves are a good even size.

Twice-baked garlic soufflés

Makes 6 individual soufflés

FOR THE SOUFFLÉS

5 tbsp butter

1 head of fresh garlic, trimmed and chopped roughly, or 5 cloves dried garlic, papery skins removed, chopped

½ tsp vinegar

1 cup milk

3 tbsp all-purpose flour

leaves from a couple of sprigs of thyme

1 cup grated Cantal, Comté or Cheddar cheese

½ cup grated Parmesan

4 large eggs, separated

FOR SERVING

1¼ cups heavy cream

seasoning, nutmeg, extra Parmesan, a few bread crumbs

You will need six ¼-cup individual soufflé dishes

Melt 1 tbsp of the butter and add the garlic, ¼ tsp salt, pepper to taste, ¾ cup water and the vinegar. Simmer covered for 10 minutes, then uncover and boil till the water has evaporated. Add the milk, bring to the boil, then process in a blender. Measure 1 cup garlic-milk mixture.

Heat the remaining butter and stir in the flour and thyme. Cook for a minute, then make a white sauce by gradually stirring in the garlic milk till thick. Transfer to a big bowl, add the grated cheese, three-quarters of the Parmesan, then the egg yolks. Set aside.

Heat the oven to 350°F (325°F convection). Butter the individual soufflé dishes and dust the sides with the remaining Parmesan; if you have any left over, stir into the sauce. Set in a roasting pan and put a kettle on to boil.

Beat egg whites till firm but not dry. Fold half into the soufflé base, then add the rest. Spoon into the dishes (fill them almost to the top), pour boiling water into the pan to one-third of the depth of the dishes and bake for 20–25 minutes, till puffed and cooked through. Remove from oven and leave to cool—they will sink.

When cool, run a knife round the edge to loosen each soufflé, gently upend on to your hand, then put the right way up on one big dish or 6 gratin dishes. (You can make the soufflés a day ahead, or even freeze them. Make sure they are at room temperature before the second baking.)

To serve, set your oven to 400°F (375°F convection). Mix the cream with salt and pepper, grated nutmeg and

Parmesan or other cheese. Pour over the soufflés to cover completely, then if you wish sprinkle with bread crumbs. Bake for 10–15 minutes, till golden and the sauce bubbling. They will gently re-puff.

MAKE IT LOOK GREAT

I like to tuck a couple of cloves of garlic confit around each soufflé as it comes out of the oven. To make this, I poach skinned garlic cloves in olive oil to cover for 20 minutes till tender. The oil the garlic has been cooked in is useful for other dishes and dressings.

From August to October we can pick everything we need for a ratatouille fresh from the garden. Although the ingredients can be stewed together, I prefer to cook them individually and arrange them in small piles on each plate in the spirit of a *dégustation*.

Deconstructed ratatouille

Serves 12

6 tbsp oil, for cooking

good handful of basil and 12 small bunches of cherry tomatoes on the vine, to serve

FOR THE DRESSING

2 tbsp sherry vinegar

1 tbsp balsamic vinegar

6 tbsp olive oil

FOR THE AUBERGINES

4 medium-size eggplants, cut into 1-inch cubes

finely chopped mint

FOR THE PEPPERS

4 yellow, orange or red peppers, or a mixture

24 pitted black olives, roughly chopped

finely chopped thyme

FOR THE ZUCCHINI

2¼ pounds zucchini (4–6, depending on size), if possible a mix of yellow and green, seeded if necessary and sliced into slivers or chunks

finely chopped rosemary

First shake together the vinaigrette, season and taste. Vinegars vary, so you may need more olive oil or more vinegar. You will not need all the dressing for this recipe.

Put the eggplant cubes in a colander over a bowl. Sprinkle with 3 tsp salt, toss thoroughly and leave to drain for a good hour, or up to 3 hours.

Meanwhile, skin the peppers. Many cooks have their favorite method, but mine is to grill the peppers, turning three or four times, till the skin is blackened and flaky all over. I then leave them in a bowl covered with a plate till cold, discard core and seeds then peel off and discard the skin. Sometimes this operation goes easily, other times it seems fiddly. Slice the pepper into long slivers, mix with the olives and thyme, add a splash of dressing and set aside.

Now return to the eggplant. Rinse the cubes well, then use your hands to squeeze them firmly to remove as much fluid as possible and put in large bowl. Toss with 2 tbsp olive oil.

Put the zucchini in another bowl and toss with 2 tbsp olive oil and seasoning. Put the eggplant in one large roasting pan and the zucchini in another and roast for 30–40 minutes at 475°F (425°F convection) till well browned and tender, tossing every 10 minutes. Set aside in bowls.

FOR THE TOMATOES

2 onions, cut into ¾-inch chunks

3 cloves garlic, crushed

6 large ripe tomatoes, skinned, cored, seeded and cut into 2½-inch pieces

about 20 capers, rinsed, dried and roughly chopped

RAYNAUDES SECRET

Chiffonades: for a zucchini risotto, make a chiffonade of zucchini blossoms in exactly the same way as the basil chiffonade in the recipe. In the morning, pick male zucchini flowers (remove stamen in the center) or pull female flowers delicately off the end of very young zucchini. Wash carefully (earwigs are common) and dry, then arrange into a pile, roll and shred.

The most exciting, which I call my Yellow Submarine chiffonade because it is psychedelic, is made by making a thick, broad pile of green basil, purple basil, zucchini flowers and nasturtiums. Roll and shred as above and use to adorn a warm salad of multicolored beetroot. A finishing scatter of blue borage or chicory flowers will convince guests they are seeing things.

For the tomatoes, heat 2 tbsp olive oil in a large deep pan and fry the onion over a lowish heat till golden, 15–20 minutes. The onion should retain some texture, but if it tastes raw continue cooking as once the tomato is added it will not cook further. Sprinkle with the garlic and cook for a couple of minutes, then add the tomatoes. Watch carefully as you cook for just 5 minutes, at which point the tomatoes will soften and release their juices. Stop at this point and transfer to a bowl.

When ready to serve, add mint to eggplant, rosemary to zucchini, capers to tomatoes. Check seasoning of each, adding a splash of dressing as necessary. Drain the peppers and tomatoes by setting in sieves over small bowls, and do the same for zucchini and eggplant if they have released liquid.

To serve, make a chiffonade of basil by piling leaves on top of each other, then rolling up like a cigar. Slip a twist tie or a rubber band around the stem end to keep in place, then slice thinly at right angles from the tip, to make a sort of confetti of basil. Put this in a bowl and dress very lightly.

Take 12 plates and put a small bunch of cherry tomatoes in the center, then a spoonful of each different vegetable in each quarter. Strew lightly with the dressed basil.

Think of a cheese soufflé made on the flat, filled with a creamy Roquefort filling and then rolled up like a jelly roll. At its most sensuous served warm, it makes a sumptuous first course or lunch or supper dish. One guest said she loved this so much she wanted to sleep with it.

Roulade of Roquefort

Serves 8 as a starter, 4–6 as a main dish

FOR THE ROULADE

3 tbsp butter

¼ cup flour

1¼ cup milk (cold)

1⅓ cups grated Cantal, Comté or Cheddar cheese

a little grated nutmeg, Dijon mustard, cayenne pepper

3 eggs, separated

2 tbsp grated Parmesan

small handful of sliced almonds

FOR THE FILLING

2 tbsp butter

2 tbsp flour

⅔ cup milk

1 tsp Dijon mustard

5–7 tbsp Roquefort cheese, crumbled

more grated Parmesan and a few extra sliced almonds, toasted, to serve

You will need a 10x13-inch pan or roasting pan, lined with parchment paper

For this dish, you make two sauces, one after the other.

Put the first three roulade ingredients in a generous saucepan (too small and it will splash). Turn the heat to medium-high and, whisking at a comfortable pace and without relenting, bring to a boil, at which point the sauce will thicken dramatically. Turn the heat to a simmer, simmer for 3 minutes, then transfer to a large bowl. Stir in the cheese, seasonings and flavorings to taste, then the egg yolks. Set aside while you make the filling (if making in advance, chill in the fridge—bring back to room temperature before using).

Make the filling from the butter, flour and milk in the same way—it will be thicker than the other sauce. Stir in the mustard and season generously but do not add the Roquefort. Press plastic wrap on the surface to prevent a skin forming. Crumble the Roquefort into a small bowl. Set aside the filling and the Roquefort (if making in advance, chill—bring back to room temperature before using).

To bake the roulade, whisk the egg whites with a pinch of salt to soft peaks. Fold into the yolk mixture and pour into the pan. Use a spatula to smooth the mixture into the corners. Sprinkle evenly with Parmesan and almonds and bake for 18–20 minutes at 400°F (350°F convection) until well puffed, golden and just firm to the touch. Do not worry if it rises unevenly or has the odd peak, like a miniature mountain range.

Remove from the oven. Lay another large sheet of baking paper over the top of the cooked roulade and put a large board on top of that, then invert the whole thing. Lift off the pan and peel away the parchment paper. You now have the roulade on a piece of parchment paper on a board.

Spread the roulade with the filling and scatter evenly with the Roquefort. Use the paper to help you roll up tightly from one of the long sides like a jelly roll. Leave wrapped in the paper for up to 10 minutes.

At this point, if you are accompanying with salad (see below), put this on each plate. Remove the paper from the roulade and slice thickly on the oblique. As you cut each slice, lift it using your knife, a slice or spatula on to the plate and lay on its side. It will be soft and oozy—this is correct. Serve at once.

MAKE IT LOOK GREAT

You can put the roulade on a board and serve it directly to guests, but the slices can be quite messy, so I always serve it sliced.

By a happy accident I discovered that this is wonderful accompanied by a Caesar-style salad. Use a crisp lettuce such as Little Gem or romaine, break the leaves up small and chill them in a salad bowl. Mash up 4 or 5 rinsed anchovy fillets and whisk them into 5–6 tbsp vinaigrette dressing. A shake of Worcestershire sauce and squeeze of lemon make nice additions. At the last minute, pour the dressing over the leaves, scatter generously with Parmesan and some small croutons fried in butter with garlic crushed over at the last minute, and toss.

RAYNAUDES SECRET

Lining a pan with parchment paper: cut out a piece of paper about ¾-inch larger than the pan in each direction, then fold up the sides. Roughly press the corners so they keep in place, but do not worry unduly.

Timings: you can pour the roulade mixture into the pan, scatter it with the Parmesan and almonds and leave it at room temperature for up to half an hour before baking. I put the roulade in the oven a good half an hour before we want to serve it. I take it out when it is cooked, cool it for 3–4 minutes, then turn it out, fill it and roll it up. I then leave it rolled up in its paper, keeping nicely warm, for up to 10 minutes, before slicing and serving.

This gutsy dish is where Manoir meets gastropub. It looks impressive, and more impressive still everything can be got ready ahead, and the boudin and scallop cooked in seconds at the last minute.

Seared sea scallop on boudin noir with parsley sauce

Serves 8

FOR THE POTATOES

4 potatoes, peeled and cut up

2 tbsp butter

few tbsp hot milk

FOR THE SAUCE

¼ cup heavy cream

2 cloves garlic, finely chopped

handful of parsley

TO FINISH

8 slices boudin noir or black pudding

8 scallops, with coral

Cook the potatoes in gently boiling salted water till soft—gentle bubbling is better than ferocious boiling. Drain well and return to the hot pan (off the heat) to dry off completely. Transfer the potatoes to a ricer or sieve and press back into the pan. Beat in the butter and milk to make a rich, ultrasmooth purée and season well.

Divide among 8 gratin dishes, or spread over base of 1 large gratin dish. If doing this in advance, cover with plastic wrap to prevent it from drying out.

To make the sauce, simmer the cream with the garlic and reduce till thickened and saucelike, about 10 minutes. Blanch the parsley in boiling water for 30 seconds, drain and plunge into iced water to fix the bright green color. Squeeze dry with your hand, then process in a blender with the reduced cream.

When ready to serve, heat the potato in a warm oven. Heat the sauce, either over hot water or in a small pan.

In a hot frying pan, dry-fry the boudin noir until browned on each side—30 seconds to 1 minute per side. Nest a slice on each mound of potato and keep warm. Season the scallops. In the fat in the pan over a high heat, brown for 1 minute per side.

Spoon a little sauce over the boudin noir. Top each slice with a scallop and drizzle with the rest of the parsley sauce, then serve at once.

Scallops usually come with a small crescent-shaped tendon attached to one side. This toughens when cooked, so is best removed. Run your finger round the edge till you find it and gently peel it away.

RAYNAUDES SECRET

This elegant and unusual soup is an excellent amuse-bouche served in coffee cups, or a luxurious starter to open a dinner party.

Fennel soup with goat's cheese

Serves 4, or 8 miniatures in cappuccino cups

4 bulbs of fennel, washed, trimmed and fronds set aside

2 cloves garlic, peeled and trimmed

1 cup chicken stock or milk

6 tbsp goat's cheese, cut up or crumbled

1¼ cups heavy cream

about 2 tbsp butter

little grated nutmeg

a squeeze of lemon, splash of Pernod (optional)

Slice the fennel in quarters and steam with the garlic for about 25 minutes, till completely tender.

Put in a pan with the stock or milk, bring to the boil and cook gently for 5 minutes, adding the cheese a minute before the end. Process in a blender for a full minute until totally smooth, then return to the pan with the cream, butter, nutmeg and plenty of seasoning.

Now check the seasoning. If the soup tastes too creamy, add some lemon. If it tastes bland, add salt and pepper, a little at a time. If it lacks character, add just ½ tsp Pernod (it will contribute an aniseedy background note, and should not be identifiable). If the soup is too thick, thin judiciously with milk or water. When ready to serve, heat the soup till hot, but avoid boiling.

MAKE IT LOOK GREAT

To accompany this soup, I like to make a miniature *croque-monsieur* by toasting triangles or rectangles of bread, spreading lightly with a little butter and a touch of Dijon mustard, and topping with a slice of ham and crumbled goat's cheese (this needs to cover the ham completely or the edges of the ham will curl up like a day-old sandwich). I slip this under the broiler till golden. Either float the *croques* in the bowls of soup, or put alongside the coffee cup.

RAYNAUDES SECRET

Goat's cheese in France varies from very fresh and wet (for instance the Petit Billy brand) to distinctly mature and dry. Our local cheesemonger at Carmaux has a wide selection (many from the Loire). He says that his British customers prefer it at the medium-fresh stage, and his French at a drier and more mature stage.
You can use either for this soup, but I usually go for a medium-dry, log-shaped goat's cheese from Le Pic in the north of the Tarn. A Sainte-Maure from Touraine would be a good alternative—another logshape, which makes for easy trimming.

I was taught this dish by a country house cook in Britain years ago, but it was two years before we could serve it at Raynaudes because it took that long to get horseradish established in the garden. It is one of our most popular and unusual dishes.

Fillet of Dover sole in horseradish sauce

Serves 4 as a light lunch dish, 6 or 8 as an appetizer

4 skinned fillets from 2 medium-size Dover sole

1¼ cup milk

FOR THE SAUCE

4-inch piece fresh horseradish, cleaned and scraped

1 small spring onion, trimmed

2½ tbsp white wine vinegar

1 tbsp granulated sugar

good pinch of mustard powder

⅔ cup heavy cream

large handful of parsley and chives, very finely chopped

Cut each fillet down the center to make two, so you have 8 slim fillets in total. To cook the fish, lay the fillets in one layer in an ovenproof dish. Season lightly. Heat the milk to boiling and pour over, cover with foil and slip into a 400°F (350°F convection) oven for about 7 minutes, till just tender when prodded with the tip of a sharp knife. Remove and allow to cool under the foil.

To make the sauce, process the horseradish in a blender until pulverized—your eyes will water when you take the lid off. You will need about 1½ tbsp—set aside the remainder for the moment. Add the spring onion, vinegar, sugar, mustard and plenty of seasoning and blend again, scraping down the sides as necessary. Transfer to a small bowl and stir in the cream gently. Taste carefully—it is likely to need more salt. Add more horseradish if you wish. The sauce will thicken as it stands. (And will also, of course, go beautifully with a roast of beef.)

Lift the cooled fish from the milk and lay in a shallow dish. Pour over the horseradish sauce and shake gently so it covers the fillets. Sprinkle copiously with the herbs and leave in the fridge till about half an hour before serving. For a light main course, serve 2 fillets each; for an appetizer, 1.

MAKE IT LOOK GREAT

For our *dégustation* evenings we present a fillet in the center of the plate with a tiny salad to one side, and a spoonful of herring caviar to the other.

Although most Raynaudes dishes are firmly rooted in the cooking of southwest France, we follow the example of French friends and neighbors in making culinary forays into DOMTOM (*départements et territoires d'outre mer*—French colonies, ex-colonies and dependencies).

Lemongrass-coconut soup

Serves 4

large piece of galangal, thinly sliced

large piece of fresh ginger, thinly sliced

12 kaffir lime leaves

4 lemongrass stems, trimmed, bashed and sliced into 2-inch lengths

1⅔ cups chicken stock

1⅔ cups can unsweetened coconut milk

TO FINISH

1 chicken breast, trimmed and cut into bite-size pieces

14-ounce can of Chinese straw mushrooms, drained and halved, or ¼ pound fresh mushrooms, trimmed and quartered or thinly sliced

Last year an enterprising Vietnamese woman opened a food shop in Albi, selling fresh Asian ingredients—and this simple but fragrant soup is, for us, the result. Roti— Asian flatbread—is the ideal accompaniment, and if you keep a clear head can be cooked at the same time as you are finishing the soup.

Up to an hour or two in advance, simmer the first 6 ingredients, covered, for 10–15 minutes. Leave to steep until ready to finish the soup. Don't be alarmed if the coconut milk appears to separate at this point.

RAYNAUDES SECRET

Roti is a simple flatbread we make to accompany this dish. Hand-mix a wettish dough of 1⅔ cups all-purpose flour, ¾ cup plus 1 tbsp whole wheat flour, 2 tsp sugar, 1½ tsp salt and 1 cup warm water with 2 tsp fresh yeast (see page 220 if using dried). Leave to rise for an hour or hour and a half, then flour your work surface liberally—the dough is sticky—and roll out very thinly. Brush lightly with melted butter, roll up like a giant jelly roll and cut into 8 or 10 buns. Flatten each one with the palm of your hand and put side by side on a well-floured piece of parchment paper in the fridge until ready to cook. At this point heat a frying pan or griddle, roll out each roti to about ⅓-inch thick, brush with more butter and cook about 2 minutes per side till golden and puffed.

TO SERVE

3 spring onions, trimmed and finely sliced

2 tbsp lime juice

2 tbsp Thai fish sauce

large handful of fresh coriander (cilantro)

very finely sliced red chilli, to pass round separately

Meanwhile, prepare the chicken and mushrooms and put in a bowl in the fridge, and put the spring onions, lime juice and fish sauce in another bowl. Wash and dry the coriander and chop, up to an hour before serving.

Shortly before serving, strain the soup base into a clean pan. Bring to a simmer and add the chicken and mushrooms. The moment the chicken is cooked—just 3–5 minutes—remove the pan from the heat. Add the spring onion mixture and the chopped coriander. Mix well, ladle into bowls and serve, passing the chilli round separately for guests to add if they wish.

You can make a surf-and-turf version of this soup by adding one-half pound of prawns with the chicken. Use any type you like, as long as they are shelled, cleaned and bite-size.

MAKE IT LOOK GREAT

In summer we adorn this soup with a twisted blade of fresh lemongrass, for squeezing and sniffing.

Main Courses and Side Dishes

Spiced PORK BELLY *with* onion confit

The ultimate roast PORK TENDERLOIN

Fresh *SPÄTZLE*

Crisp roast DUCK *with* olives

SADDLE OF LAMB stuffed *with* Agen prunes *and* rosemary

BREAST OF PIGEON *with* Armagnac jus

Straw potato cakes

Seven-hour LEG OF LAMB

TARTE TATIN of Belgian endive

Roast FILLET OF VEAL in a Parmesan crust

Glazed QUAIL FILLETS *with* pomegranate pilaff

Pommes dauphinoise

Roast POLENTA wedges

Chervil RISOTTO

Caramelized potatoes

Crushed new potatoes

Pork belly has always featured on the Raynaudes menu, and although I have gradually refined the recipe, it still involves a long slow stretch in the oven that fills the kitchen and courtyard with tantalizing aromas. If possible, season the meat 3 days ahead.

Spiced pork belly with onion confit

Serves 4–6

2¼ pounds pork belly

FOR THE SEASONING MIX

1 tsp coriander seeds, dry toasted in a pan

½ tsp fennel seeds

½ tsp coarse salt

plenty of black pepper

FOR THE ONION CONFIT

8 medium onions, sliced

1 bulb fennel (optional), trimmed and sliced

½ tsp ground cloves

If available, buy pork belly with the skin on. This will later be sliced off and used as crackling. If the bones and cartilage are intact on the underside, they can be removed and discarded when the belly has been cooked.

Score the skin of the pork in rough diamonds to stop it buckling and shrinking in the oven. Grind the coriander and fennel seeds and add the salt and pepper. Rub over all the sides of the pork. Refrigerate till ready to cook—for up to 3 days.

Mix the onion, fennel and cloves and select a roasting tin or gratin dish no larger than the pork belly. Pile in the onions, season and put the pork, skin-side up, on top. The dish or pan may appear absurdly full, but the onions will drastically reduce in volume as they cook.

Roast at 350°F (325°F convection) for 1½ hours. As the pork shrinks, periodically stir the onions and push them underneath the meat to prevent them scorching. Turn the heat down to 275°F (250°F convection) and continue roasting, stirring the onions occasionally, for a further 2½ hours (4 hours in total). You can make ahead up to this point and set aside if you wish.

RAYNAUDES SECRET

Choosing the right size pan or dish for a recipe can make or break it. As a general rule, bigger is better: there is nothing messier or more irritating than trying to cook things in pans that are too small, or whisking mixtures in bowls that are overflowing. But in this case, smaller is better: both the onions and the pork shrink enormously, and onions that are not covered by the meat stand a strong chance of being scorched.

About half an hour before serving, remove the onions to a small sieve and drain off the fat. Slice the crisp skin off the pork in one piece (to make crackling), leaving as much soft fat on the pork as possible, and lightly score this fat once again. If the pork has bones or cartilage on the underside, gently pull or cut them out and discard. Put the pork and the crackling side by side in the pan or dish and finish roasting for 20–30 minutes at 400°F (375°F convection), by which time the fat on top of the pork should be light golden and the crackling supercrisp.

Reheat the onions briefly. Slice the meat thinly across the grain and serve on top of the onions.

Buying meat in France

Different butchering methods make meat-buying in France a potential minefield. After many puzzling and frustrating experiences, I found in *Larousse Gastronomique* what I had been waiting for—diagrams of pork, veal, beef and lamb showing exactly how the beasts are butchered in France, Britain and the United States. (Note that the different nationalities of animals appear to have different facial expressions.)

A brief glance at the diagrams informs you that French butchering is more detailed and complicated than the others, resulting in a wider range of cuts, each with its own name. For instance, a rib of beef in France is divided into four different cuts (*hampe, plat de côtes couvert, plat de côtes découvert, poitrine*).

BEEF

Many British gourmets and cooks find French beef disappointing. The main offender is the *entrecôte* steak (from the rib), which is often so tough and tasteless as to be uneatable.

One difference from British is that French beef is never hung, a process that develops flavor and tenderness. The reason for this is apparently economic—hanging meat is a rich man's game, it makes it more expensive. It must be done in controlled conditions, and after hanging the meat must be sold promptly. Fresh, unhung meat has a far longer window in which to be sold.

Of course with certain cuts and dishes this does not make a significant difference. Fillet of beef is very tender whether hung or not. Slow-cooked cuts do eventually become tender, though you may need to add an hour to the cooking time.

A few cuts that can cause confusion. *Faux-filet* is sirloin. *Gîte* is leg or shin. *Bavette* is flank, used for frying or stewing.

VEAL

French veal is mainly what is termed in Britain "rose veal," from beasts 4–5 months old. In our region at least, the beasts are loose-boxed and raised with their mother. The greatest delicacy is the fillet or *filet mignon*, which can be roast or cut into steaks. It benefits from being barded with fat, or breaded before roasting (as on page 158), to keep in the juices.

Other noteworthy cuts, apart from the obvious escalopes, are *quasi* (the back tip of the fillet) and *jarret* (shin, for osso buco). The widely sold *tendron* is breast.

LAMB

French lamb prices fluctuate widely according to season, though they are generally higher than in Britain. Most supermarkets also stock frozen lamb from New Zealand of extremely good quality. *Gigot* is the leg, *souris* the shank. The top section of a *gigot* consists of a fleshy cushion, which if you are lucky you can buy separately, called *selle* or saddle—this is one of the great gourmet treats at Raynaudes, slow braised and stuffed with Agen prunes and herbs (see page 148). A *carré* of lamb (literally, square) is usually cut from the neck or best end of neck.

PORK

French pork has a delicious flavor and is excellent value. The *filet mignon* is the fillet or tenderloin, quick cooking and tasty. *Echine* is blade or rib, often rolled for roasting. It is not always as tender as the loin (which is usually sold simply as *rôti de porc*) but has more flavor and is less inclined to dry out. *Poitrine* is belly. *Jambon* and *jambonneau* are leg cuts, often including the hock.

If you ask for *poitrine*, incidentally, specify *poitrine fraîche* for belly. *Poitrine salée* is cured belly (can be used very thinly sliced as streaky bacon) and *poitrine fumée* smoked belly (smoked streaky).

DUCK, CHICKEN AND OTHER BIRDS

Canard is duck and *canard gras* a duck that has been raised for foie gras. The latter will have a very thick layer of fat round the meat making it look like an avian Sumo wrestler. This is traditionally the duck to use for confit and for long slow cooking. *Canette* is a duckling.

As well as ordinary chickens, you often encounter a *coq* or very large *poule* for making soup or boiling (do not be tempted to use for *coq au vin*: too tough). The French are very partial to other birds, *dinde* (turkey), *pintade* (guinea fowl), pigeon and *caille* (quail). At Christmas *chapons* (capons, neutered male birds) of chicken and guinea fowl are available, for roasting or poaching.

ORGANIC AND "RED LABEL"

Organic meat and poultry is increasingly available in France, though it is worth saying that standards of animal keeping are generally high and a lot of produce (for instance from small farms and market gardens) is organic but not certified as such.

The French are fanatical about classification and labeling schemes for everything from meat to olive oil, *jambon de pays* to jam. Look out for AOC (*appellation d'origine contrôlée*) and the prestigious *Label Rouge*, which is an indicator of top quality.

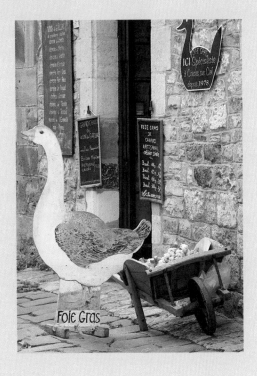

Tenderloin or fillet of pork has become an everyday cut in Britain, but treated with care and roasted whole it becomes something very special. We serve the pork fillets with a simple cherry sauce made in the pan while the pork is in the oven, and *spätzle* (see recipe and picture overleaf).

The ultimate roast pork tenderloin

Serves 6–8

6 juniper berries,
6 peppercorns, 1 dried red chilli (all optional)

2 tbsp salt

6 tbsp granulated sugar

2 pork tenderloins

hoisin sauce

FOR THE CHERRY SAUCE

about 40 ripe cherries, pitted

1 cup stock

½ cup *crème fraîche* or heavy cream

squeeze of lemon juice

splash of kirsch (optional)

When guests ask how we have cooked the pork to make it so tender and succulent, I usually give the credit to the tastiness of French pigs, but there is more to it than that. The secret is brining the tenderloins for a couple of hours by immersing in a salt-and-sugar solution.

The spices give an extra depth of flavor, but are not necessary if you are in a hurry. If using them, crush them lightly and put in a pan with about 1 cup water. Bring to the boil and leave to steep for 10 minutes, then stir in the sugar and salt. Transfer to a bowl or large plastic container of at least 1 gallon capacity and add 1 quart of water. Stir to dissolve. If you are not using spices, just dissolve the salt and sugar in the water.

Trim the fillets carefully. It is worth taking extra trouble to find the silverskin—a thin membrane covering parts of the fillet—and peel it off. Cut any obvious bits of fat away at the same time.

Immerse the pork in the brine (which should be roughly at room temperature) and put in the fridge for 2 hours.

At this point lift out the pork (throw away the brine), rinse thoroughly and dry well with paper towels (you will need lots). Do not season.

Heat a frying pan and add a little olive oil. Brown the fillets, both at once, turning frequently, for a total of about 5 minutes (they will only go a pale brown on account of the brine). Transfer to a roasting pan (no need for a rack), paint lightly all over with hoisin sauce and roast for about 16–18 minutes till a probe thermometer inserted in the thickest part of the fillet reads 135°F. If judging by eye, note that the brining means the pork will have a slight pink tinge, like ham.

Leave to rest, covered with foil, for 15 minutes while you finish the sauce.

To do this, add the cherries to the pan in which the pork was browned and sizzle for 3–4 minutes till just changing color. Add the stock and bubble fast for about 5 minutes till syrupy, then add the cream and continue to bubble until the thickness you require. Check seasoning. I invariably find that a sauce including cream needs a squeeze of lemon to brighten it up. A splash of kirsch— at Raynaudes we make our own—adds a glamorous extra note if you wish.

MAKE IT LOOK GREAT

Slice the pork fillet on the diagonal and pour over the sauce. The cherries are inclined to roll where they wish, but (rather like planting bulbs for a natural effect) usually look best left where they land.

Brining is little known in Britain, but is a brilliant way to make meat more tasty, tender and succulent. In the United States, for instance, many cooks brine the Thanksgiving turkey— an epic procedure considering the size of American turkeys. You can use the same brine formula, in just the same way, for chicken breasts. Simply rinse, dry and dust them in flour before frying in the usual way.

Cooking thermometer:

I cannot imagine cooking a roast of meat without one. Why rely on guesswork? Mine has a probe which can be inserted into the meat (always the thickest part) and put in the oven, and it beeps when the predetermined temperature is reached. This is just one use for it. I would not be without a thermometer in the kitchen—to temper chocolate, to check water is at the optimum temperature for mixing dough and to choose the best place for the dough to rise, and to tell me if my custards are cooked and my bread baked.

If you are a keen skier you may have encountered *spätzle* in Austria, but otherwise this speciality from Swabia in southern Germany remains a bit of a secret. It makes an interesting and accommodating alternative to potatoes, rice or pasta.

Fresh spätzle

Serves 4

1 cup plus 2 tbsp all-purpose flour (ideally cake flour for extra lightness)

grated nutmeg

2 eggs, lightly beaten

a little oil

butter for frying

You will need a colander or spätzle *press*

The principle is simple. You make a thick batter, push it through the holes of a colander into boiling water to form tiny featherlight dumplings shaped like little squiggles (*spätzle* means little sparrows in the Swabian dialect), then fry them till crisp on the outside. They pose no particular problems—they do not stick together, they do not turn to mush if you overcook them and they are made ahead (up to the point of frying). As they are light and delicate, you can eat them plain, with extra butter (or better, browned butter), herbs and melted cheese, but I think they are best as an accompaniment to meat.

The batter is simply stirred together. Put the flour in a bowl with plenty of seasoning and the nutmeg and stir in the eggs with a fork. Now add enough warm water— 2–3 tbsp—to make a very thick batter. Flour varies, so you cannot be exact: it should be thicker than pancake batter, but still liquid. You are going to be pushing it through the holes of a colander, so it wants to dribble rather than flow.

Leave the batter to stand while you put a deep, wide pan of salted water on to boil. You want as large a surface area of water as possible. I use my largest saucepan, a third full with water. A frying pan is too shallow.

When the water is boiling vigorously add a splash of oil, which will coat the little dumplings and stop them sticking. Put your colander over the water (throw away some of the water if the colander is touching it) and then spoon in about half the batter. Now quickly stir and push the mixture through the holes, trying to get it through within about 20 seconds, then lift away the colander and

Ultimate roast pork tenderloin
(see previous page) served with
spätzle.

stir to make sure the *spätzle* do not stick to each other.
Wait until the dumplings have risen to the surface of the
water, then about half a minute or minute longer, then
scoop them out (I use a small sieve) into a fresh colander
or sieve. Repeat with remaining mixture.

Transfer the *spätzle* to a lightly greased roasting pan,
shake to separate, put on a few knobs of butter and leave
to cool. Do not worry if the *spätzle* appear to clump when
cold; they will separate when reheated.

To serve, heat a knob of butter in a frying pan and fry
the *spätzle* over medium heat for about 10 minutes,
till lightly browned and slightly springy in texture.

Serve at once. Be extremely generous with your sauce
(or serve extra in a gravy boat) as they simply mop it up.

It is said that France is divided into three regions of gastronomy determined by the fat it uses for cooking. In the north, this is butter. In the southeast, olive oil. In the southwest, it is unquestionably duck fat.

Crisp roast Duck with olives

Serves 4

1 duck, about 4 pounds

FOR THE SAUCE

2 cups homemade chicken stock

1 tbsp tomato purée, dried herbs, fennel seeds, bay leaf

⅔ cup pitted green olives

This recipe yields a succulent roast duck, every morsel of which is tender and tasty, and as a by-product, a good half pint of duck fat. No cook worth her salt would waste a scrap of this precious substance, which is kept in a pot in the fridge and used for frying and flavoring.

Trim any flaps of fat on the duck, and pull out any lumps of fat tucked inside. Rinse and dry the duck, then prick lightly all over with a skewer (about 20–30 times), trying to pierce the skin but not the flesh underneath. Rub all over with salt and sprinkle some inside the cavity.

Put on a rack and roast upside down for 3 hours at 250°F (200°F convection). Drain the fat into a bowl, set the duck the right way up and increase the heat to 350°F (325°F convection) for 45 minutes longer, till nicely browned. Leave to stand for 15 minutes, loosely covered with foil.

Reduce the chicken stock with the tomato and herbs to a saucelike consistency, then strain into a clean pan. Simmer the olives in water for 2 minutes to temper the flavor, then strain and stir into the sauce.

Cut the duck into pieces and serve with the sauce.

RAYNAUDES SECRET

Baked olives: it is a revelation how olives are transformed by heating, their flavor mellowed and softened. Next time you wish to serve olives with drinks, try baking them. Cut a square of foil and put in a small baking dish, pulling up the sides. Put rinsed olives in the middle with a splash of olive oil, half a dozen peppercorns, a halved clove of garlic, a few coriander seeds, a bay leaf and a strip of orange zest. Wrap in the foil to enclose the olives completely then bake at 350°F (325°F convection) for 10 minutes or up to half an hour. Serve in the foil parcel.

This has become a Manoir favorite. I use the local *pruneaux d'Agen*, which taste riper and fruitier than ordinary prunes. Saddle of lamb is delightfully simple to serve: simply cut off the strings, slice and serve with the reduced cooking juices.

Saddle of lamb stuffed with Agen prunes and rosemary

Serves 3–4

2 tbsp olive oil

1 shallot, finely chopped

1 clove garlic, crushed

8 pitted prunes, preferably *pruneaux d'Agen*, roughly chopped

1 tbsp chopped rosemary (or mint)

1 saddle of lamb, bones removed and set aside

FOR THE BRAISING MIXTURE

1 onion, sliced

1 carrot, sliced

1 glass red wine

1 head garlic, kept whole, papery outside removed, top cut off horizontally

2 bay leaves

squeeze of lemon, to finish

You will need a small, tightly lidded braising pan that will accommodate the lamb and vegetables without too much extra room to spare, and cooking string

After carving countless legs of lamb for Manoir dinners, I began to realize that the most delicious and succulent part of the leg is at the top. I asked my butcher about this. He explained that this part has a name—*selle* or saddle—and, after some persuasion, agreed to sell it to me separately. If you can persuade your butcher to sell you the saddle, ask him at the same time to remove (but give you) the small bones to leave a roughly rectangular piece of meat weighing from 1⅛ pounds to 1¼ pounds. This is spread with stuffing, rolled up tightly and tied into a small cylindrical parcel with string.

Heat half the oil in the braising pan and fry the shallot over a moderate heat till golden—about 4–5 minutes. Scatter over the garlic and fry for 30 seconds. Transfer to a bowl and mix with the prunes and herbs. Season and leave to cool. Do not wash up the braising pan.

Lay the lamb saddle out on a board, skin-side down. It should be roughly rectangular. If the meat is particularly thick in some parts and not others, cut into the thick part (but not right through) to form a flap. Rehearse rolling it up from one short side to the other, to make a small tight roll. Try it in the other direction—one will normally seem easier and result in a neater parcel.

Season the meat and use a spatula to press the stuffing all over it, pushing it into flaps but leaving a narrow border all round. Roll tightly and tie with string. Season the skin side.

Add the other tbsp of oil to the braising pan and sear the lamb over a high heat until it is well browned all over— about 5 minutes in all—turning frequently. Remove to a small bowl while you brown the onion, carrot and reserved bones over a high heat, turning frequently— another 5 minutes.

Pour in the wine and cook quickly to reduce to a syrup. Now put in the lamb saddle, nestling it comfortably among the bones and vegetables, and add the garlic and bay leaves. Add water so that about a third of the lamb is immersed in liquid and bring to the boil. Cut or tear a piece of parchment paper the shape of the pan, press down well over the lamb and vegetables to keep everything moist, clap on the lid and put in the oven heated to 325°F (275°F convection). After 20 minutes check the lamb is gently simmering and adjust heat if necessary. Braise for between 1¾ and 2¼ hours, turning twice, until the meat is tender right through. When cooked, remove from the oven and leave covered—the meat will remain hot for 45 minutes.

About 10 minutes before serving, strain the cooking juices into a container—I use my gravy separator (leave the meat to keep warm in the braising pan). Discard vegetables except for the head of garlic. Put the defatted juices into a pan, squeeze in the garlic, which will be meltingly soft, and boil the sauce fast till reduced to the desired consistency. Taste, and if necessary brighten the taste with a squeeze of lemon. Serve the meat in slices with the sauce

---

RAYNAUDES SECRET

Stuffing and tying roasts of meat: I always recommend a short rehearsal. With larger roasts—for instance, boned shoulder or boned leg—you are faced with several choices, so run through them and decide before you start stuffing and tying.

I have tried different sorts of cooking string and for me chunky works best. You can see exactly what you're doing and it does not cut into the meat. It is easy to ensure you have removed it all before serving. I am not gifted at knots, or remembering how to do them, but if you are interested, you will find an idiot-proof photographic guide in Judy Rodgers' *The Zuni Café Cookbook*. Worth having for this alone—except that the recipes are utterly brilliant too.

Make Perfect Stock

When guests compliment me on how tasty the food is at Raynaudes, it is usually down to our homemade stock. Many of our main courses and 90 percent of our sauces are stock-based—stock is to my cooking as a double bass is to a jazz trio.

When I lived in a London loft and worked in the BBC offices at White City, making my own stock was not practical or neighborly, so I bought the best substitutes I could find. Powdered stock from Switzerland under the Marigold brand, or mild-flavored fresh stock from the refrigerated section. Though useful I do not believe these are any substitute for the real thing.

You can make stock in a large batch—though not too large, as the operation gets unmanageable—and freeze it. I find it convenient to measure the stock at the time of putting into freezer bags—1 cup, 2 cups and 4¼ cups—so I can defrost the right amount.

CHICKEN STOCK

I use 3⅓ pounds mixed chicken wings, drumsticks and thighs, cut up at the joints and put in a roasting pan with a sliced onion and sliced carrot. Roast at 400°F (375°F convection) for about 30 minutes, till well browned, then transfer with juices to a large stock pot or pressure cooker. Pour over a glass of red or white wine and reduce to a syrup by fast boiling, then cover with cold water. Bring to a boil, skim and add about a dozen peppercorns, 2 bay leaves, sprigs of thyme and other herbs, fresh or dried. Simmer for an hour and a half, semi-covered, or boil at full pressure for 45 minutes in a pressure cooker. Strain, pressing

juices out of cooked chicken and vegetables, cool and skim off fat.

For pigeon or quail stock, use the carcasses of the birds (having cut off the breasts to serve for a main course). No need to brown them in the oven; brown them instead with the vegetables directly in a little fat in the stock pot or pressure cooker, scrape up the nice burnt bits on the bottom thoroughly when adding the wine, and continue as above.

VEAL AND BEEF STOCK

Classically, veal stock is simply boiled, without the meat and bones being browned first, but I find this insipid and I prefer it made exactly like beef stock.

Take about 3½ pounds shin of beef or veal with bones. Cut the meat off the bones and put together with an onion and a carrot in a large roasting pan. Roast at 400°F (375°F convection) for about 30 minutes, till well browned, then transfer with their juices to a large stock pot or pressure cooker. Pour over a glass of red wine and reduce to a syrup by fast boiling, then cover with cold water. Bring to a boil, skim and add about a dozen peppercorns, 2 bay leaves, sprigs of thyme and other herbs, fresh or dried. Simmer for 2 hours, semicovered, or boil at full pressure for 90 minutes in a pressure cooker. Strain, pressing down well on cooked meat and vegetables, cool and skim off fat.

DEFATTING STOCK

Stock always has fat that needs removing. I have a gravy separator that I bought from John Lewis in London—the larger you can find, the more useful it will be. Otherwise use a large container and either skim carefully, or (better) chill and remove the fat when the stock and/or fat have set solid. You can speed this operation up by putting the stock in the freezer.

To transform stock into jus

Homemade stock can be turned into the best of all sauces, a simple but luxurious jus, by reducing in a large wide saucepan till boiling with small tight bubbles and syrupy in thickness (allow 15–30 minutes).

Some recipes ask you to reduce stock by half in which case the traditional method is to measure the height on a wooden spoon, and continue till the height is halved. I do not find this reliable or convenient, so, if quantity is critical, I transfer it to measuring cup and check it that way.

A meat jus needs little adornment. Check for seasoning—it is unlikely to need salt. Add a splash of Armagnac for depth of flavor, or lemon juice or balsamic vinegar to brighten it up. If it tastes too meaty or bony, a splash of Madeira or Marsala will sweeten it.

You can go one step further and turn a jus into a luxurious butter-thickened sauce. Take ½ cup jus, reduced from stock as described. Add a squeeze of lemon juice. Turn the heat to just below a simmer and keep it there while you whisk in, over the course of about 5 minutes, 12 tablespoons chilled butter cut in cubes, added one by one. The sauce will get thicker and glossier as you do so. Check seasoning at the end—I find a final splash of Armagnac raises it to sublime heights.

French pigeons are young, juicy, fresh and bred for the table—like American squab. In the southwest, every house worthy of the name has a *pigeonnier*, either built in (as at the Manoir) or detached.

Breast of pigeon with Armagnac jus

Serves 6

3 plump young pigeons, cleaned

FOR THE JUS

a little duck or goose fat, or vegetable oil

1 medium onion, carrot and stick of celery, roughly chopped

1 bay leaf

splash of Armagnac

2½ tbsp chilled butter (optional)

TO COOK

a little duck or goose fat, or olive oil, or clarified butter

Using a small sharp knife, cut the breasts off the pigeons, keeping the skin on (just as you would remove a chicken breast, but on a smaller scale). Flatten with the palm of your hand, season well all over and refrigerate covered until ready to serve.

Discard any liver and entrails in the carcasses (I find they make the sauce taste too strong) and cut the remainder (skin and bones) up as best you can using a heavy knife or poultry shears—aim for pieces no bigger than about 2 inches. Use to make pigeon stock as on page 150, defat, then reduce to a jus.

To cook the pigeon, heat the duck fat or oil till smoking and put in the pigeon breasts skin-side down. Cook for 2 minutes (if they are burning turn down the heat), then the other side for 2 minutes longer. Check the doneness with a knife—they should be medium rare, with a hint of blood. Rest in a low oven, or tented with foil, for 5–10 minutes before slicing into 2 or 3 and serving with the jus (mounted with optional butter), on a crisp straw potato cake (see overleaf).

MAKE IT LOOK GREAT

Like duck breasts, pigeon can bleed rather unattractively on to the plate in the short period before being conveyed to the table. If this worries you, the solution invented by Andonis, chef-proprietor of nearby hotel Le Cuq-en-Terrasses, is to mask it in a ruby-coloured sauce—perhaps by stirring red currant jelly, or fresh myrtles, into the pigeon jus above.

I have tried dozens of different potato accompaniments, from *rösti* to potato baskets, but this is the simplest and best.

Straw potato cakes

Serves 6

2 medium potatoes, shredded into tiny matchsticks, using a mandoline or julienne slicer

1 shallot, chopped very finely

duck or goose fat, olive oil or clarified butter

Because there is only me in the kitchen cooking dinner, dishes have to be practical and achievable. This potato dish is so quick that it can be made while the meat rests. A few hours in advance you can peel the potatoes and julienne them; keep them under water.

When ready to cook, drain the potatoes thoroughly and squeeze as dry as you can on a towel—twisting and wringing as much as possible. Mix with the shallots and plenty of seasoning.

Heat 2 tbsp fat in a large frying pan and put in 3 handfuls of potato, shaping as rough circles. Moderate the heat if necessary, but after 3–4 minutes they should have started to stick together and the underside to go brown. Flip them over using a palette knife or spatula and cook the other side the same way. They will not be very tidy or regular, but they will taste delicious.

Keep warm on a baking sheet and repeat with the next 3, adding a little more fat to cook in if necessary (usually it isn't). Serve as soon as possible.

Of all the recipes I created during my time at *BBC Good Food* magazine, this is the one that most people seem to remember. It is in fact an old French favorite, sometimes called *gigot à la cuillère* (lamb with a spoon) because it is so meltingly tender.

Seven-hour leg of lamb

Serves 6

1 large leg of lamb, about 6½ pounds

4 onions, sliced

4 carrots, sliced

8 cloves garlic, peeled but left whole

1¼ cups white wine

1¼ cups stock

2 tbsp Armagnac, to finish

You will need a tightly lidded braising pan in which the lamb is a close fit. If you have a round braising pan rather than oval, it is a good precaution to ask your butcher to saw the shank bone, without detaching it, so you can bend it back and fit it in the pot.

Season the lamb and heat the braising pan on the stovetop. Brown the lamb on all sides thoroughly, so it is nicely scorched—about 10 minutes. It will not brown during braising, so this is your only chance. Lamb varies, so add a little oil if the pan seems dry, and pour away most of the fat if a lot has collected in the pan during the browning.

Lift out the lamb and set aside. Add the onions and carrots and brown these—about 5 minutes—then add the garlic, lamb, wine and stock. Season and bring to the boil. Cut out a piece of parchment paper the same size as the pan and lay over the lamb to keep it moist.

Transfer to an oven heated to 250°F (200°F convection) and cook for 7 hours, turning twice. After 5 hours the meat will be cooked; you can serve it now, or stick with tradition and give it a couple of hours more.

There is no need to rest the meat when it is cooked this way, but you need to finish the sauce. If you are planning to serve the meat on a dish, put it on the dish now. Use wide spatulas and arrange your serving dish in the most convenient spot before attempting to lift the extremely tender lamb out of its cooking pot. If you are planning to serve it in the cooking pot, drain all the cooking juices into a bowl.

Strain the juices—I discard the vegetables now but you can serve them—and defat them (I use my gravy separator). Put the juices in a pan and boil quickly to reduce to a saucy consistency. Stir in the Armagnac, if you wish. Pour over the lamb or serve alongside.

Beautiful Belgian endive is piled high year-round in French markets and greengrocers, and I love to find ways to use it. Everyone adores this unusual and ritzy main course—especially vegetarians.

Tarte tatin of Belgian endive

FOR THE PASTRY

1⅓ cups plus 1 tbsp all-purpose flour

a little cayenne pepper

5 tbsp butter

½ cup Parmesan, grated

FOR THE FILLING

4 medium carrots, cut into small batons

1½ tbsp butter and 2 tsp olive oil

½ tsp sugar

3 heads of Belgian endive, trimmed and cut in half lengthwise

4 tbsp white wine or sherry

1 tsp thyme leaves, finely chopped

2 tsp brown sugar

2 tbsp balsamic vinegar

1⅛ cup grated Comté, Cantal or Cheddar

You will need a solid-based cake pan of 10–12-inch diameter, or an ovenproof frying pan of about the same size

Make the pastry first by whizzing the flour, seasoning and a pinch of cayenne pepper in the processor. Add the butter, whiz to crumbs, then the Parmesan and whiz to mix. Now with the machine running, dribble in enough water—about 2 tbsp—to bind the mixture into a ball. Turn out, press into a disc and chill.

Cook the carrots in boiling salted water until almost tender. Melt half the butter with the oil in a frying pan, sprinkle with the sugar and add the endive, cut-side down. When it is brown (about 5 minutes), turn it over and brown the other side (about 3 minutes). Add the wine, 4 tbsp water and the thyme to the pan. Reduce heat to low and simmer covered for 10 minutes, till the endive is almost tender. Add the carrots. Turn the heat up and boil the juices until reduced to a syrup, another minute or 2. If baking in the same frying pan, remove the carrots, endive and juices and set aside.

Put the remaining butter in the pan (or baking pan, if using) and melt over direct heat. Add the brown sugar and vinegar and cook together to caramelize. Off the heat, arrange the endive cut-side down in the pan, the carrots and their juices. Cover with the cheese. Set aside.

Roll out the pastry to slightly larger than the pan. Lay out over the filling. Cut off any major excess, then tuck in the edge all round.

Bake for 25–35 minutes at 400°F (350°F convection), till pastry is golden and cooked through. Run a knife round the edge, then invert on to a large plate and serve at once.

Braised Belgian endive can be made by the same method. Melt 1 tbsp butter with 1 tsp oil in a frying pan, sprinkle with ½ tsp sugar and add 3 or 4 halved heads of endive, cut-side down. When it is brown (about 5 minutes), turn it over and brown the other side (about 3 minutes). Add 4 tbsp wine, 4 tbsp water and chopped thyme to the pan. Reduce heat to low and simmer covered for 10 minutes, till the endive is completely tender. Boil the juices, uncovered, until reduced and finish by whisking in an extra tbsp butter, 1 tsp lemon juice and finely chopped parsley.

Raynaudes is in the heart of the Ségala region, famed for its veal. Of all the cuts, the fillet or *filet mignon* is the most choice—just slightly paler than beef, with a sweet flavor and toothsome tenderness. The crust keeps the veal extra juicy.

Roast fillet of veal in a Parmesan crust

Serves 8

3½ pounds fillet of veal

1 egg, beaten

2 anchovy fillets, mashed

1 clove garlic, crushed

1⅓ cups fine soft fresh bread crumbs

¼ cup grated Parmesan

Depending on which end of the fillet the butcher has given you, your veal may have a flap, or be tapered. You are aiming for a roughly tubular shape, so use a couple of skewers inserted lengthwise to achieve this, pinning the flap into place, or doubling back the point and securing. Season well.

Mix the egg, anchovy and garlic and brush all over the veal (discard excess)—the anchovy, used to make the crust adhere, is not tasted as anchovy, just a general savoriness, but can be omitted. Mix the crumbs and Parmesan and press over the veal until completely covered on all sides. Put on a rack in a roasting pan and allow to come to room temperature.

Heat oven to 400°F (350°F convection). Roast the veal for 40–50 minutes, till it is medium rare and internal temperature taken in the thickest part of fillet is 125°F. Leave to rest for 20–30 minutes, loosely tented with foil, before carving into thin slices.

We serve this with a veal jus (see page 151) or wild mushroom sauce (see left) and pommes dauphinoise (see page 163).

RAYNAUDES SECRET

Wild mushroom sauce: to accompany the veal, fry ½ cup mixed wild and cultivated mushrooms in a knob of butter till brown. Add a finely chopped shallot and lightly brown, then stir in 100ml of red or white wine and 1¾ cup veal stock. Bring to the boil and strain into a clean pan, reserving the mushrooms. Boil to reduce to ⅔ cup. When ready to serve, keep sauce at a low simmer and gradually beat in 12 tbsp chilled butter cut in pieces, till thick and glossy. Add mushrooms, heat through and serve.

The classic French treatment for quail and pigeon is to roast the birds whole in a very hot oven and let guests pick off the delicious morsels of meat. At Raynaudes, however, we like to make life as easy as possible for guests, so whenever possible the boning is done in the kitchen.

Glazed quail fillets with pomegranate pilaff

Serves 4

6 whole quail

FOR THE QUAIL STOCK

a little duck or goose fat, or vegetable oil

1 medium onion and 1 carrot, roughly chopped

1 bay leaf

FOR THE GLAZE

3 pomegranates

1 tbsp lemon juice

1 clove garlic, minced

FOR THE PILAFF

1 cup basmati rice, rinsed and drained

1 bay leaf

1 tbsp olive oil

1 onion, chopped

¼ tsp ground cumin

¼ cup walnuts, toasted in the oven and chopped

1 scallion, thinly sliced

bunch of coriander (cilantro), chopped

Remove the fillets from the quail and make stock from the remains of the birds (having thrown away any innards) following the method on page 150. Defat the stock before using.

Cut one of the pomegranates in half and use a small spoon to remove the seeds, discarding any of the bitter white pith. Set aside. Squeeze the other two pomegranates using a lemon squeezer so you have about 1 cup juice. Boil in a pan to reduce to ¼ cup and stir in the lemon juice and garlic.

Take 2 cups of the quail stock (save the rest for another use) and put in a pan with the bay leaf. Bring to the boil, add the rice and cook till tender, about 10–12 minutes, then drain and set aside. All this can be done in advance.

When ready to cook, brush a roasting pan with a little oil and brush the glaze all over the quail fillets. Put in the pan and roast for 10–15 minutes in a 350°F (325°F convection) oven, reglazing at half time—check they are just done with a small sharp knife. Set aside, loosely tented with foil.

For the pilaff, heat the oil in a frying pan and gently fry the onion for 6 minutes till soft but not colored, then add the cumin and the rice. Heat gently, stirring for about 5 minutes, then stir in the walnuts, scallion, most of the coriander, pomegranate seeds and salt to taste.

Put the pilaff on plates and arrange the quail on top, scattering finally with a little more coriander.

Pomegranates are a brilliant pantry standby as they keep for ten days in a cool place. Picking the jewellike seeds out from the pith is a bit fiddly but once done the seeds keep in the fridge for a couple of days—excellent to liven up a fruit salad or to put in the juicer with apples for a breakfast health juice.

Champagne sauce and grapes are the perfect accompaniment to quail in early to midsummer, when the pomegranate season has a hole in it. Fillet the quail in exactly the same way. Fry them for 3–5 minutes, turning once, in a little duck or goose fat or oil in a large frying pan and set aside in a warm oven. Without washing or wiping the pan, fry halved, seeded grapes for 3–4 minutes, then deglaze with a glass of champagne. Bubble fast to reduce to a syrup, add some chicken (or quail) stock and reduce again to a saucy consistency, and stir in a little cream or *crème fraîche*. Check seasoning and add a squeeze of lemon if it tastes too creamy. Serve the quail fillets with sauce poured over—excellent with Crushed New Potatoes (page 170).

I must have tried more than twenty different methods of making everyone's favorite potato dish, and this is the best.

Pommes Dauphinoise

Serves 6–8

1 large clove garlic

2 cups milk or half milk, half cream

1 tsp salt

plenty of black pepper, ground nutmeg and a pinch of cayenne

2 pounds potatoes, sliced as thinly as possible (processor is ideal)

1 cup grated Cantal or Comté cheese (or Cheddar) (optional)

If baking in a dish, cut the garlic in half and rub the dish with it, then crush the garlic and put in a large saucepan. After a few minutes, when the garlic-rubbed dish has dried, butter the dish well. If baking in a pan, line with parchment paper or foil (foil will need buttering), and simply crush the garlic directly into the saucepan.

Add all ingredients except the cheese to the saucepan and bring to a boil. Stirring continuously, to prevent the potatoes sticking, simmer for a minute or two until the liquid thickens perceptibly, then remove from heat. If using cheese, stir half in now. Pile into the dish or pan and push the potatoes down into the liquid so they are not sticking out. If using cheese, sprinkle the remaining half on top.

Bake for 45 minutes to an hour at 350°F (325°F convection) until the top is dark golden and the potatoes completely tender when poked with a knife (the thinner you sliced the potatoes the quicker they will cook).

MAKE IT LOOK GREAT

Pommes dauphinoise is essentially a farmhouse dish, and though we do not seek geometrical perfection at the Manoir dinner table, it can look a bit untidy on the plate. The neatest way to serve this dish is to bake it in advance in a pan lined with parchment paper (choose a smaller pan for thicker portions of dauphinoise, larger if you prefer thinner). When cold, remove the potatoes from the pan either by lifting with the paper or sliding out, and cut into round, square or rectangular portions. Arrange, spaced apart, on fresh parchment paper on a baking sheet and reheat for 10–15 minutes till sizzling.

RAYNAUDES SECRET

Perfect dauphinoise: this recipe is the fruit of two great breakthroughs. The first was slicing the potatoes as thinly as possible, on a mandoline or with the fine slicer on the food processor. This means the potatoes absorb flavor right to the very center. The second was heating the potatoes with the milk and cream before piling them into the dish (see previous page). This makes the cooking far quicker and more reliable, and the result more moist and flavorful.

Polenta can be a boring ingredient—it is what you do with it that counts. I am not claiming this recipe is Italian or authentic, but we serve it to delicious acclaim with chicken, guinea fowl or quail.

Roast polenta wedges

Serve 4–6

1 tbsp olive oil and 1 tbsp butter

1 onion, chopped finely

1 clove garlic, finely chopped

2 tbsp finely chopped rosemary

1 cup cornmeal

½ tsp salt

2⅛ cups milk

1½ tbsp butter and 5 tbsp grated Parmesan, plus extra if necessary

Heat the olive oil and butter in a large thick-based saucepan and fry the onion until golden—about 7 minutes. Stir in the garlic, cook for 30 seconds, then remove from the heat and stir in the rosemary.

Now stir in the cornmeal, salt and milk. Return to the heat and whisk constantly as the polenta comes to the boil. Change to a wooden spoon when the mixture becomes too thick and continue to beat constantly. Turn down the heat to minimize spitting, and boil for about 5 minutes, stirring frequently. Taste to check the polenta is no longer gritty.

Stir in the butter and the Parmesan, taste carefully (it must not be bland, so add more salt and cheese if necessary and plenty of ground black pepper), and pour on to a chopping board. Use a spatula to level it into a rectangle of about ½-inch thickness but do not flatten the top too much—grooves and swirls are fine. You can do this up to 6 hours ahead—refrigerate when cold.

When ready to serve, cut the polenta into long wedges and set on a baking sheet lined with parchment paper. Brush with olive oil. Roast for 30 minutes at 275°F (250°F convection) or 20 minutes at 350°F (325°F convection) or 10 minutes at 400°F (350°F convection). When ready they should be gently sizzling and lightly crisp on the edges, but not brown.

Bits of bacon, fried with the onion, make a tasty addition to this recipe, and sage or thyme works as well as rosemary. Extra ingredients should be cut up finely or they make it difficult to slice the polenta into wedges.

RAYNAUDES SECRET

Cornmeal is a confusing ingredient, not least because it is sometimes labeled polenta (which is technically the name of the cornmeal once it is cooked). I use a cornmeal described as quick cooking and medium ground; I have tried others (instant, ordinary and stoneground, which is pleasingly flecked with black) but I have not found they behave especially differently—you will know they are cooked when they lose their gritty texture

This risotto makes a delicious emerald-green accompaniment to roast veal and confit of guinea fowl.

Chervil risotto

Serves 6–8 as an accompaniment

1 tbsp olive oil and 1 tbsp butter

1 onion, finely chopped

1 clove garlic, crushed

1¼ cups Carnaroli or Arborio rice

1 glass dry white wine

1 bay leaf

1 quart chicken stock, simmering gently in a pan

3 tbsp butter and ½ cup grated Parmesan, plus extra for serving

FOR THE CHERVIL OIL

4–5 bunches fresh chervil (or parsley)

1 cup olive oil

1 clove garlic, roughly chopped

Make the chervil oil first by whizzing the herbs, oil, garlic and seasoning in a blender. You will need 3 tbsp for this recipe—keep the rest in a jar in the fridge for a week or freeze.

Make the risotto in the classic way. In a roomy pan, heat the oil and butter and fry the onion until soft but not golden, about 5 minutes. Add the garlic, stir for 30 seconds, then stir in the rice. Stirring constantly, fry the rice until the grains start to look opaque round the edges (but do not brown them)—about 4 minutes on a medium-high heat. Pour in the wine and reduce over a fast heat till syrupy. Throw in the bay leaf.

Risotto making: you can scale this recipe up or down as follows—1 cup rice to 2⅔ cups stock, 1¼ cups rice to 3⅛ cups stock, 2½ cups rice to 6⅓ cups stock. Only add the last installment of stock when you are sure the rice will need it.

Can you make risotto in advance? Well, up to a point. Follow the steps through cooking the onion and garlic, toasting the rice and reducing the wine. At this point, add one third of the total stock, bring to a boil, turn off heat and cover. Leave for several hours undisturbed—the rice will set in an apparently solid mass. When ready to cook, add almost all of the remaining stock in one go, bring to the boil and simmer for 10 minutes, stirring from time to time, adding the remaining stock if necessary. Take care in the last few minutes and test constantly.

Carnaroli rice gives a better result than Arborio when using this method—it is more forgiving if you cook it a minute too long. The cook-ahead method is also convenient when making a saffron risotto—stir in a good pinch of toasted saffron filaments when adding the first third of stock and leave to infuse with the rice.

Set a timer for 18 minutes—the rice will probably need 20. Now start adding the simmering stock, ladle by ladle. Aim to keep the rice just covered by stock at all times, and stir more or less constantly, keeping the liquid simmering. Depending on the surface area of your pan and exact regulation of heat, you may not need all the stock or you may need a little more. At 18 minutes check the consistency of the rice and cook for 2 further minutes if necessary. It should be firm but with no hint of crunch or stickiness.

When the rice is done, turn off the heat and remove the bay leaf. Stir in the butter and then the Parmesan, followed by 3 tbsp of the chervil oil. Taste to check seasoning and leave for a full 5 minutes to rest.

Ladle on to plates or bowls and serve with extra Parmesan sprinkled on top. If serving by itself, as a starter, finish with a dribble of extra chervil oil, or lemon-scented olive oil, which we buy from the shop Oliviers & Co (O&Co).

This unusual potato dish—originating in Scandinavia—goes beautifully with strong, richly flavored meats. Although it sounds as if it might be a sweet dish, the caramel turns the potatoes dark, with an almost bitter, chicorylike finish.

Caramelized potatoes

Serves 4–6

1½ pounds new potatoes, or small potatoes

3 tbsp granulated sugar

1 tbsp butter

1¼ tsp salt

Cook the potatoes in their skins in boiling water until just tender. Cool and slip off the skins. Cut into halves or wedges.

Take a large frying pan and add the sugar. Wait for the sugar to melt, then cook it, stirring occasionally, until it melts to a dark gold color. Add the butter and salt, stir until melted, then add the potatoes. At first it will appear a disaster—the caramel will clump around the potatoes—but carry on cooking gently and stirring for 12 minutes (trying not to break up the potatoes), by which time the potatoes will be gloriously coated and glistening. Serve at once.

This trendy side dish is a crunchy halfway house between roast and sauté potatoes. Small potatoes (no need to peel) are boiled till tender, squashed with the palm of your hand, allowed to cool, then half an hour before eating, roasted till crisp and sizzling.

Crushed new potatoes

Serves 4

olive oil, butter or goose fat

12–16 small potatoes, red or white

2½ tsp salt, plus coarse salt to serve (optional)

Line a roasting pan with parchment paper and brush with olive oil, butter or fat (to give a roasty finish to the potatoes; the parchment paper is there to make light work of cleaning up afterwards). If making double quantities, use 2 roasting pans so the potatoes are well spread out. Scrub the potatoes (do not peel) and put in a pan with 2 tsp of the salt and water to cover by 1 inch. Boil for about 20 minutes, till completely cooked but not falling apart. Drain in a colander, and when cool enough to handle but still hot, put on a board. Gently squash each potato until it is about ¼-inch thick, trying not to break it up (though it doesn't matter if there is the odd casualty). Arrange in one layer in the pan, brush with more oil, season with the remaining salt and set aside to cool. You can do this an hour ahead, but if longer, refrigerate when cold.

When ready to cook, heat oven to 425°F (400°F convection) oven. Bake for 30–40 minutes till golden, flipping potatoes at half time and checking the seasoning is to your liking. Serve hot, sprinkled with a little coarse salt if you like.

RAYNAUDES SECRET

The finest new potatoes I have encountered in France come from the Atlantic coast. The first are from the Ile de Ré, near La Rochelle, then (with an even better flavor) from Noirmoutier, a little further north. They arrive in shallow wooden boxes, which later prove very useful in the garden for collecting soft fruits, herbs and edible leaves.

Desserts, Petit Fours and Chocolates

Raspberry-cinnamon streusel TART

Lemon pot de crème

Strawberry surprise birthday BOMBE

Toasted almond PANNA COTTA *with* jelly of Gaillac doux

Apple-cinnamon CROSTATA

Coeur à la crème | Chocolate nirvana

Dark *and* deadly chocolate MOUSSE

Fresh blackberry MOUSSE

The ultimate strawberry TARTLETS

Peach-almond CRUMBLE | Celebration chocolate LOG

Peaches in Gaillac Doux

Deconstructed Black Forest GATEAU

Black currant leaf SORBET | Raynaudes vanilla ICE CREAM

Chocolate FONDANT | Limoncello

After-dinner BROWNIES | Fresh mint TRUFFLES

Choc-walnut-Armagnac FUDGE | Millionaire mendiants

MACARONS au chocolat | Cocoa-nib FLORENTINES

Homemade vanilla MARSHMALLOWS

One of the most popular of all our desserts at Raynaudes, this is a cross between a crumble and a cake. Two things make it extra special when eaten on the Manoir terrace—beautiful homegrown raspberries from the fruit garden, and the exotic spiciness of Sri Lankan cinnamon from the spice lady at Carmaux market.

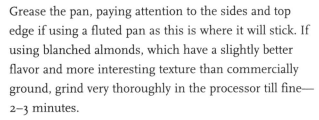

Raspberry-cinnamon streusel tart

Serves 6–8

1¼ cups blanched or ground almonds

10 tbsp softened butter

¼ cup superfine sugar

1 cup plus 3 tbsp self-raising flour

1–2 tsp cinnamon

1 egg

½ pound raspberries

confectioners' sugar

crème fraîche or sabayon ice cream, to serve

You will need a 14x4-inch fluted pan or a 8-inch loose-based tart pan, in either case 1½-inch deep, or 8-inch loose-based or springform cake pan

Grease the pan, paying attention to the sides and top edge if using a fluted pan as this is where it will stick. If using blanched almonds, which have a slightly better flavor and more interesting texture than commercially ground, grind very thoroughly in the processor till fine—2–3 minutes.

Now process the almonds with the butter, sugar, flour, cinnamon and egg till combined. Set half aside (if you have time, put in a bag and freeze). Spread the rest in a layer in the base of the pan, using a wet fork. Cover with raspberries and then crumble or grate over the reserved mixture. It does not have to cover completely.

Bake for 40–60 minutes at 350°F (325°F convection) oven. The top should feel firm but springy and be well browned; if it begins to scorch before you feel the torte is cooked, cover with foil after 40 minutes. Serve dusted with confectioners' sugar, accompanied by *crème fraîche* or ice cream: sabayon ice cream is especially good.

Sabayon ice cream

A frozen take on the French sabayon, or Italian zabaglione—not too creamy but decidedly alcoholic. To make about 3⅛ cups, heat 1 cup milk, ½ cup plus 2 tbsp sugar, 4 egg yolks and ½ tsp cornstarch in the microwave, as in the recipe on page 200. When the mixture has thickened, stir in 1 cup cream, 6 tbsp Marsala, 2 tbsp dark rum and 1 tsp vanilla extract. Chill to almost freezing and then churn in an ice-cream maker.

There are easier recipes for this favorite French dessert, but I have never discovered one with silkier texture or greater depth of flavor. The key is to bake them till just set. If you overdo it the dessert will not be ruined but it will be more custardy.

Lemon pot de crème

Makes 8 pots

finely grated zest of 4 lemons and ¼ cup lemon juice

¾ cup plus 2 tbsp granulated sugar

3⅓ cups heavy cream

10 egg yolks

2 tsp vanilla extract or seeds from ½ vanilla pod

You will need eight ¼-cup ramekins

Heat the oven to 325°F using the conventional (nonconvection) setting (cooks the custards better and does not blow the foil round the oven like a kite). Put the ramekins in a roasting pan and put on the kettle so you have boiling water to hand.

Make a lemon syrup by combining zest, juice and about one-third of the sugar. Simmer for about 15 minutes till reduced to about ½ cup. Set aside.

In another pan, heat the cream and another one-third of the sugar till just boiling. Whisk the egg yolks with the remaining sugar in a bowl and continue whisking as you pour in a good ladleful of the hot cream. Return the yolk mixture to the saucepan and heat gently for 3–4 minutes till it thickens slightly—if you have a thermometer it should read 170°F. Stir in the (unstrained) lemon syrup, mix well, and strain into a large lipped container. Add the vanilla, stir well and pour into the ramekins.

Pour boiling water to a third or halfway up the sides of the ramekins, lay a sheet of foil loosely over the top and bake for about 25 minutes. Check the custards by gently shaking them. When cooked, the custards should be lightly set, not liquid. If you have a thermometer, the centers should be 150°F (do not worry about making a hole in the custard, it will close up). If some of the pots are ready before others, lift out and put the rest back for about 7 minutes, and retry. They should all be cooked by about 35 minutes—if not, increase your oven temperature by forty degrees and remember for next time.

Cool the custards in the pan in the water then refrigerate, lightly covered. Serve with whipped cream (see below) and a tuile cookie (see pages 231–33).

MAKE IT LOOK GREAT

It is gilding the gingerbread, but I like to top mousses, custards and ice creams with a rosette of crème chantilly. My formula is very simple: whip 1 cup heavy cream with 1 tbsp superfine sugar and 1 tsp vanilla extract till stiff. Spoon or pipe as required. This will keep in the fridge for up to an hour, or longer if you store it in a small sieve over a bowl, so liquid that leaks out can drain.

EARL GREY POT DE CRÈME

The Manoir for some reason attracts a lot of guests from the northeast of England, and when they visit I sometimes make Earl Grey pot de crème in their honor (Earl Grey being a Northumbrian). To make 4 pots de crème, follow the same method. Heat 1 cup heavy cream and 1 cup milk with 2 tbsp Earl Grey tea leaves and leave covered for 30 minutes. Reheat till boiling and remove from heat. Whisk 4 egg yolks with 6 tbsp sugar, ½ tsp lemon zest and a pinch of salt, then mix this into the hot milk-cream-tea mixture. Strain into a lipped container, pressing well on the tea leaves to extract the flavor, pour into the ramekins and bake as above.

Ramekin size: when I first started making desserts at Raynaudes, I used to get in a dither about whether or not a recipe would yield enough mixture to fill 8 ramekins, and what about if I wanted to use ramekins of a slightly different capacity, and make 6 bigger desserts, or 10 slightly smaller. This is not so much of a problem as you think. Simply fill the ramekins of your choice to two-thirds full, then distribute the remainder among them (obviously if you have too much, make an extra to have tomorrow). They do not have to be full to brimming, but you do want them all to be roughly the same size.

Based on a recipe from Californian cook Alice Waters, this recipe makes a stunning birthday dessert-cake. You need to prepare it the day before.

Strawberry surprise birthday bombe

Serves 12–15

FOR THE SPONGE

5 eggs, separated

½ cup cold water

½ tsp vanilla extract

½ tsp almond extract

1¾ cups superfine sugar

1 cup cake flour

½ tsp baking powder

¾ tsp cream of tartar

FOR THE FRUIT

1¼ pounds fresh strawberries

⅓ cup plus 1 tbsp granulated sugar

1 tsp bourbon or brandy

2 cups heavy cream

FOR THE SYRUP

2 tbsp granulated sugar

5 tbsp warm water

1 tsp lemon juice

2 tbsp bourbon or brandy

You will need a large baking pan (or roasting pan) about 12x16-inches and a large basin or bowl (2½–3-quart capacity)

To make the sponge, line the bottom of a pan with parchment paper. Whisk the egg yolks in an electric mixer till light and foamy (about 5 minutes), then beat in the water, vanilla, almond and sugar. Beat for 5 more minutes till mousselike. Sift the flour, baking powder and ¼ tsp salt, and in another bowl beat the egg whites with the cream of tartar to soft peaks.

Fold the flour into the yolks, then the egg whites, pour into the pan and bake at 350°F (325°F convection) for about 15 minutes, till lightly golden and just firm when touched. Cool in pan, then remove to a board. Freeze half the sponge (keep for any occasion when you need a superior sponge) and slice the other half horizontally, using a large knife, to make two very thin sheets. Do not worry if it breaks or crumbles in places.

Hull and halve or quarter the strawberries and put in a big bowl with the sugar and bourbon.

Mix the syrup ingredients together and add any juices from the strawberries.

Whip the first 2 cups cream to soft peaks and fold in the strawberries.

Line the large bowl with plastic wrap (if you wet the bowl slightly first it makes it easier), leaving a good overhang. Line completely with a layer of sponge, breaking up to get a good fit. Brush with syrup.

Fill with half the strawberry cream. Make a layer of sponge cake, brush with syrup and fill to the top with the

TO FINISH

2 cups heavy cream

3 tbsp granulated sugar

½ tsp vanilla extract

1 tsp bourbon or brandy

remaining strawberry cream. Use the remaining sponge to make a lid, brush over remaining syrup (pour any left round the edge to use completely), then enclose with plastic wrap and chill overnight.

To serve, turn out, remove the plastic wrap and cover completely with the remaining 2 cups cream whipped to soft peaks with the sugar, vanilla and bourbon.

MAKE IT LOOK GREAT

We serve this with a sparkler in the top and accompanied by the Queen of the Night's aria from Act 2 of Mozart's *The Magic Flute* ('Der Hölle Rache kocht in meinem Herzen').

Understated elegance sums up this light, trembling, just-set cream, one of the most popular of Raynaudes desserts. Not essential, but we adorn it with cubes of a simple jelly made from the local dessert wine, Gaillac doux.

Toasted almond panna cotta with jelly of Gaillac Doux

Makes 4

⅓ cup whole or sliced almonds

¾ cup milk

1 cup heavy cream

2½ tbsp granulated sugar

1½ gelatine leaves

FOR THE JELLY OF GAILLAC DOUX

1 cup Gaillac doux or other sweet white or rosé wine

2 tbsp granulated sugar

a squeeze of lemon

a splash of Armagnac

3 gelatine leaves

Toast the almonds lightly, chop and put in a saucepan with the milk, half the cream, the sugar and a pinch of salt, and bring to a simmer. Leave for about 10 minutes.

Soak the gelatine briefly in cold water, then squeeze with your hand and whisk into the still-hot milk till completely dissolved. Add the remaining cream. Pour into 4 small ramekins (not greased) and chill for at least 3 hours, or overnight. At 5 hours it will be very lightly set—almost dangerously so—overnight, firmer.

For the simple wine jelly, combine the first 4 ingredients. Soak the gelatine briefly in cold water, then squeeze in your hand and dissolve in 3–4 tbsp of the wine mixture by heating for 30 seconds in the microwave. Check the gelatine has dissolved, then whisk into the wine mixture and pour into a small loaf pan to set for at least 3 hours. Unmold by dipping for a mere second into warm (not hot) water and cut into cubes.

You can serve the panna cotta in the ramekin, or turn out either by dipping momentarily in very hot water and inverting, or by sliding a small knife round the side, inverting and—if necessary—agitating the plate and ramekin so the panna cotta drops out. Serve 3 or 4 cubes of wine jelly per panna cotta, and, if you like, a tuile cookie (see pages 231–33). In season, fresh strawberries or raspberries would be a perfect alternative to the wine jelly.

This wonderful apple tart—incorporating the best elements of a crumble—is best served with a dollop of *crème fraîche*. We make it most memorably with the first of our apple crop, Gravenstein, the fruits of which cook to melting sweetness.

Apple-cinnamon crostata

Serves 8–10

FOR THE PASTRY

1 cup plus 2 tbsp plain flour

½ tsp granulated sugar

5½ tbsp unsalted butter

FOR THE TOPPING

⅓ cup plus 1 tbsp all-purpose flour

⅓ cup plus 1 tbsp brown sugar

1 tbsp cornmeal or semolina

¼ tsp ground cinnamon

3 tbsp unsalted butter, at room temperature

⅓ cup sliced almonds

Make the pastry in a food processor by whizzing the flour, sugar and a pinch of salt, then adding the butter in cubes till the mixture is the consistency of bread crumbs. Add up to 3 tbsp water to bind. Form into a shallow disc, wrap in plastic wrap and refrigerate.

Make the topping in a small bowl. Mix flour, sugar, cornmeal, cinnamon and a pinch of salt, then fork in the butter till crumbly. Stir in almonds and set aside.

Prepare the apples by mixing the sugar with the vanilla seeds (the seeds are inclined to stick together, so do this thoroughly to get rid of clumps). Mix with the peeled, sliced apples and butter. All this can be done in advance.

To assemble the crostata, roll out the pastry on a large floured nonstick silicone mat or parchment paper. If the pastry is very cold, be patient or you will end up with a map of Newfoundland. Aim to make a thin disc, with slightly ragged edge, about 13 inches in diameter. Leaving a 1½-inch border all round the edge, arrange the apples in the center, mounding gently. Use a bench scraper to fold the edge up over the filling all round, mitering and tucking as necessary. Slide the crostata, still on its paper, on to a rimless baking sheet. (The juices can leak from the crostata and make an awful mess of the oven, so it is worth putting a rimmed baking tray underneath the

RAYNAUDES SECRET

Crème fraîche is obligatory for this dessert. To serve it in a bowl, open the pot of *crème fraîche* and drain the whey that will have settled at the bottom of the pot. Now use a spatula to turn the cream into a small bowl—it will take on its own natural sculptural form. Alternatively, add a dollop to plates, or make quenelles by scooping a spoonful of *crème fraîche* in one spoon and using another identical one to shape it into a sort of triangular section football shape. Slide on to each dessert plate beside the crostata.

FOR THE APPLES

6 tbsp granulated sugar

seeds from a vanilla pod

4 large eating apples, peeled
and thinly sliced

2 tbsp butter, melted

TO FINISH

1 tbsp melted butter

1 tbsp granulated sugar

a little confectioners' sugar

*You will need a large rimless
baking sheet for the crostata*

crostata to catch them. But you do need the crostata itself
on a rimless tray in order to slide it off when it's done.)

Brush the folded-up edge with the remaining butter and
sprinkle with sugar. Sprinkle the topping over the apple
filling to cover completely. Bake at 400°F (350°F convection)
for 40 minutes, till apples are tender and the crostata dark
golden. Leave to cool for 20 minutes then slide on to a board.
Serve warm or cool, dusted with confectioners' sugar.

You will not regret investing in a set of *coeur à la crème* dishes, as this is the most captivating of summer desserts, and can be varied all season according to what fruits are available.

Coeur à la crème

Serves 6

¾ cup mascarpone (to make your own, see page 189)

½ cup cream cheese (such as Philadelphia)

½ cup superfine sugar

1⅓ cups crème fraîche

⅓ cup plus 1 tbsp plain yogurt

soft fruits and confectioners' sugar, optional, to serve

You will need 6 small china perforated heart-shaped coeur à la crème *dishes, or one large heart-shaped dish, and enough muslin or cheesecloth to double-line them*

I am amused when guests comment how light the cream is—this is pure sleight of hand, as the ingredients are extremely rich. If you are serving this, skip the cheese course.

The aim is to whip the white ingredients into a smooth homogenous cream. Process the mascarpone, cream cheese and sugar, then briefly whiz in the other ingredients, scraping down sides of the processor.

Line the molds with wet muslin or cheesecloth, leaving enough to fold over the top so they are completely enclosed, and place them in a rimmed dish or tray. (The muslin can be put through the washing machine and reused, but it does shrink, so the first time you use it cut it out very generously to allow for this.) Mound up the filling in the molds—it will gently sink as it drains– and set the tray aside in the fridge for about 8 hours. Then remove and carefully invert the molds, peel away the muslin, and serve surrounded with fruits. Dust with confectioners' sugar if you wish.

MAKE IT LOOK GREAT

If you would like to make a little fruit sauce to drizzle round the fruit, purée ¼ pound of fresh berries with 1 tbsp of syrup (in France you can buy bottles of cane syrup, or make your own by simmering an equal weight of water and sugar for 5–10 minutes). Check flavoring and correct with more syrup or a little lemon juice. When presenting the dessert, put the coulis around the base of the heart, not on to it (to avoid the operating-theater look).

This is an impeccable flourless chocolate cake. Glazed and served in slices, it makes a glamorous finish to a dinner party or celebration meal. We also use a round cutter to create miniature cakes for our Deconstructed Black Forest Gateau (page 198).

Chocolate nirvana

Serves 12 generously

2⅔ cups chopped 70% chocolate

1½ sticks (12 tbsp) unsalted butter

5 large eggs

1 cup plus 2 tbsp superfine sugar

1½ tsp vanilla extract

¼ cup cocoa, sifted

FOR THE GLAZE (OPTIONAL)

⅔ cup plus 2 tbsp chopped 70% chocolate

2 tbsp plus 2 tsp unsalted butter

You will need a 9-inch cake pan, lined with parchment paper, buttered all round and dusted with cocoa

Melt the chocolate and butter (such as in a measuring cup or bowl in the microwave, or see page 211) and stir till smooth.

Whisk the eggs, sugar, vanilla, good pinch of salt and 2 tbsp water in a food mixer till foamy, pale and doubled in volume—about 2 minutes. Reduce the speed and pour in the chocolate mixture. Add the cocoa and continue to mix for 30 seconds. Pour into the pan and bake for 40–45 minutes at 300°F (275°F convection) oven, till a skewer inserted into the cake comes out looking wet with small clumps (like a brownie)—do not overcook. Allow to cool—it should sink and contract slightly—then remove from pan and chill.

If glazing, melt the butter with the chocolate and spread over the cake, leaving a ¼-inch border unglazed around the edge. Leave to set.

MAKE IT LOOK GREAT

Like most dense and sticky cakes, this is best sliced using a knife well heated in a cup of boiling water, then wiped dry before each slice.

White chocolate crème anglaise makes a special accompaniment. An easy way to make this is to mix 4 egg yolks with 3 tbsp sugar, 1⅓ cup milk and ½ tsp cornflour. Microwave at 1-minute intervals till it begins to thicken, whisking frequently, then at 30-second intervals until the mixture is thick and smooth. Stir in ½ cup plus 1 tbsp white chocolate till smooth and chill. Serve the cake in delicate slices in a small pool of white chocolate crème anglaise.

A grown-up mousse for lovers of 70 percent chocolate. You can make this a day ahead. For larger numbers, a fabulous and subtle addition is the blackberry mousse overleaf: half fill glasses with chocolate mousse, allow to set, then top up with blackberry mousse (recipe follows).

Dark and Deadly chocolate mousse

Makes 8 small mousses

1¾ cups chopped 70% chocolate

2 tbsp cocoa

2 tbsp superfine sugar

1 tsp Trablit coffee essence, or instant coffee powder

1 tbsp brandy

3 large eggs, separated

1 tbsp granulated sugar

1 cup heavy cream

You will need eight ¾-cup ramekins

Melt the first five ingredients in a large bowl with 7 tbsp water in the microwave and stir till smooth. (It may seem bizarre to add water to the chocolate but it is necessary to prevent the chocolate going stiff and grainy.)

Whisk egg yolks with half the remaining sugar (that is, 1½ tsp) for a minute or so, then whisk into the chocolate.

Whisk the eggs whites till frothy, add the final 1½ tsp sugar and whisk till soft peaks form. Fold into the chocolate mixture.

Finally whip the cream to soft peaks and fold this into the chocolate mixture till no white streaks remain. Spoon into the ramekins and leave to set for at least 2 hours.

MAKE IT LOOK GREAT

Decorate with a little whipped cream and chocolate shavings, made by running a potato peeler down the sides of chocolate bar, or curls (see page 196).

We have an extremely prolific blackberry, 'Thornfree', which gives us a full six weeks of juicy berries. When we get bored with making jam, this ravishingly mauve, lusciously flavored mousse takes over.

Fresh blackberry mousse

Serves 6–8

1⅛ pounds fresh blackberries, or a mixture of blackberries and raspberries

¾ cup plus 2 tbsp superfine sugar

1 tsp lemon juice

3 large eggs, separated

2 tsp powdered gelatin

pinch of cream of tartar

⅔ cup heavy cream

You will need six to eight ¾-cup ramekins

Process or blend the fruit with about a third of the sugar, the lemon juice and a pinch of salt, then sieve into a large bowl. Throw away the debris in the sieve.

Put the egg yolks in a small microwave-safe bowl with another third of the sugar and a ladleful of the berry purée. Mix well, then microwave in 15-second bursts till thickened. Whisk into the remaining purée and put into the freezer to chill.

Put ¼ cup water into a small cup and sprinkle over the gelatine. Leave for 5 minutes, then microwave in 30-second bursts till fully dissolved. Whisk into the berry mixture and return to freezer to chill.

Whisk the egg whites with the cream of tartar (which helps stabilize the mixture) till foamy, then add the final third of the sugar and whisk to soft peaks. In another bowl (but no need to wash up the beaters) whisk the cream to soft peaks. Take the berry mixture from the freezer and pour the whipped whites and cream on top. Fold all together till no white streaks remain and transfer to ramekins. Put in the fridge to set firm, about 4 hours.

MAKE IT LOOK GREAT

We top this with a little whipped cream and a frosted mint leaf. To make this, wash and dry small perfect mint leaves. Brush them very sparingly with beaten egg white (a small stiffish brush is best) then dredge each side with granulated sugar. Leave to dry on a plate for 8 hours.

Buying Dairy Products in France

British people who come to France often have trouble buying the dairy products they are used to—especially cream. Here are the major sources of confusion.

BUTTER

Most French households use *doux* (unsalted) for all purposes. Semi-salted (*demi-sel*) or salted is available and is usually used to accompany charcuterie or crudités.

MILK

Frais means fresh. You may well have to hunt it out, as only the British seem to buy it and most milk is UHT or sterilized. *Lait cru* is unpasteurized.

CREAM

The big problem for many British cooks in France. *Crème fraîche* is a cultured cream with a fresh, slightly sour taste. You can stir it into sauces, though it lacks bulk and may turn the sauce watery, and you can just about whip it, if well chilled, to a rather floppy whipped cream. You may need to adjust flavoring because of its slight sourness, and it is nowhere near as stiff as whipped British double cream. *Crème fraîche légère* is low in fat with a yogurty taste and I do not use it for cooking.

Nothing is available in France to replace British double cream, with its very high 42% fat content. The nearest is *crème fleurette* (avoid the lower-fat *crème légère* version) at about 30% fat—a light whipping cream. American cooks should use heavy cream, preferably with 40% butterfat, if you can find it. To whip this, chill everything—the cream, the beaters, the bowl—and use an electric whisk. Because the cream seems to flick round the kitchen, I put the bowl in the kitchen sink and do the whisking there. After 5 minutes of beating you will have a rather fluffy, foamy whip. I do not recommend the *crème chantilly* powder that is sold in sachets to make cream firmer.

BUTTERMILK

If you wish to use this for scones, soda bread or other baking recipes, look for Elben or other makes of *lait caillé*.

CREAM CHEESE

The ubiquitous St Moret cheese does not behave like classic Philadelphia cream cheese (which I have never seen in France) when cooking, so I substitute mascarpone. If you have a favorite cheesecake recipe you will need to experiment.

RAYNAUDES SECRET

Make your own mascarpone: boil the zest of a lime, 2½ cups heavy cream and a vanilla bean for 5 minutes, until the cream separates. Add the juice of a lime and ½ tsp citric acid (powdered, from a pharmacist) and simmer for a minute, then strain into a container. Leave for 5–8 hours, then drain in a sieve lined with wet muslin or cheesecloth overnight.

This pastry is so good you can eat it like a cookie. Everyone imagines it must have a host of ingredients to give its supreme nutty crunch, but not so. The secret is in the Demerara sugar . . .

The ultimate strawberry tartlets

Makes 6

FOR THE PASTRY

¼ cup plus 2 tbsp self-raising flour

3 tbsp all-purpose flour

1 stick (8 tbsp) unsalted butter

2 tbsp Demerara sugar

TO FINISH

6–10 tbsp mascarpone, cool but not straight from the fridge (to make your own, see page 189)

confectioners' sugar, to taste

few drops of vanilla extract

½ pound strawberries, not too big, halved

You will need a marble slab or large flat board

If serving for dinner, make the pastry in the morning or afternoon. Mix the flours with a good pinch of salt and rub in the butter (can be done in the food processor). Mix in the sugar until the mixture comes together into a crumbly ball. Shape into a squared-off sausage and refrigerate for about an hour until just firm.

Cut the pastry into 6 chunks and on a lightly floured surface roll out each to a thin circle about 4 inches in diameter. For a professional finish use a cutter to perfect the circle. Transfer to an ungreased rimless baking sheet using a spatula or palette knife and bake at 350°F (325°F convection) for 10–15 minutes until lightly golden (neither pale nor actually browned) and just firm when you touch it.

Remove from oven, count to 10 and with extreme care slide a palette knife under one of the pastry discs. Tilting the tray, slide-push the pastry disc on to the marble slab. Continue with the other discs. Nudge the discs lightly while cooling a couple of times so they do not stick to the slab or board. Leave there, covered with plastic wrap, till ready to serve.

Have ready 6 serving plates. Beat the mascarpone to soften, sifting in a little confectioners' sugar and vanilla to taste. It needs to be spreadable: too warm and it will be in danger of curdling when you beat it; too cold and it will tear the pastry when you spread it. Spread on to the pastry discs, right to the edge, then top with a tight layer of halved strawberries and a dusting of confectioners' sugar.

You can dress up this dish further by using a lemon cream instead of mascarpone. Make some lemon curd by bringing to the boil ¼ cup plus 2 tbsp sugar, the juice of 2 lemons, 5 tbsp unsalted butter and 1 tbsp finely grated lemon zest, and then whisking into 3 large beaten eggs. Return to pan and cook gently for about 5 minutes, till thickened and 160°F. This keeps for a week in the fridge. For this recipe, fold about ½ cup of lemon curd into ½ cup whipped cream and spread on the tartlets before adding strawberries.

RAYNAUDES SECRET

The vanilla extract I can find in France is variable in quality, so I have found a way to brew my own from vanilla beans. Instead of burying them in sugar (nice idea but not enough vanilla flavor for me) I put them in a jar and keep them covered with bourbon (you could also use brandy). The resulting vanilla-bourbon is not as strong as extract but a tbsp or two gives a luscious richness and depth to whipped cream, custards and ice creams.

The Midi-Pyrenees is known as the garden of France, and in midsummer your eyes will pop out at the overflowing market stalls of peaches and apricots. Our neighbors spend the hottest weeks of the year stashing this goodness away in jars, and we also like to capture the moment with juicy fruit desserts, such as this fragrant, almondy crumble.

Peach-almond crumble

Serves 6–8

FOR THE FILLING

5 or 6 peaches, peeled, pitted and cut into wedges (see page 197)

⅓ cup plus 1 tbsp granulated sugar

1¼ tsp cornstarch

3–5 tsp lemon juice (3 for peaches that are slightly unripe, 5 for fully ripe peaches)

cinnamon and nutmeg

FOR THE CRUMBLE

1 cup plus 2 tbsp all-purpose flour

¼ cup granulated sugar, plus 1 tbsp for topping

⅓ cup brown sugar

2 tsp vanilla extract

6 tbsp butter, softened

⅔ cup sliced almonds

You will need a 8-inch square baking dish

Toss the peaches and sugar together in a bowl and leave for 30 minutes for the juices to run. Tip into a colander over a bowl to catch juices. Take ¼ cup of the juices and mix with the cornstarch, lemon juice, spices and a pinch of salt. Mix with the peaches and put in the baking dish.

To make the crumble (which can be done ahead and kept in a storage container), combine the flour, sugars, vanilla and ½ tsp salt in the processor and pulse till combined. Add the butter and half the nuts and process till rough and crumbly, about 30 seconds. Add the remaining nuts and whiz once or twice just to mix. Turn out on to a rimmed baking sheet lined with parchment paper. Bake at 350°F (325°F convection) oven for 15–20 minutes, till lightly browned and firm.

When ready to cook, slide the topping off the paper over the peaches, breaking it up lightly to give a more or less even layer. Sprinkle with remaining sugar and bake at 375°F (350°F convection) for 25–35 minutes, till the fruit is bubbling. Cool for at least 15 minutes before serving with *crème fraîche* or—as at Raynaudes—sabayon ice cream (see page 174).

MAKE IT LOOK GREAT

You can make this in individual gratin dishes—they look more delicate if you are quite sparing with both fruit and crumble, and arrange them off center, to leave room for a last-minute scoop of ice cream.

This gleamingly impressive chocolate cake is worthy of the finest Parisian pâtisserie. It is made in several stages and cannot be hurried, so I prefer to make it the day before eating.

Celebration chocolate log

Serves 12

FOR THE BASE

⅔ cup plus 2 tbsp chopped 70% chocolate

⅓ cup dark brown or Demerara sugar

¼ cup (4 tbsp) unsalted butter

½ tsp grated orange zest

¼ tsp coarse salt

2 eggs

2 tbsp granulated sugar

1 tbsp flour

½ cup hazelnuts, toasted, skinned and roughly chopped

FOR THE MOUSSE

1 cup plus 1 tbsp chopped 70% chocolate

½ cup plus 2 tbsp chopped milk chocolate

1½ cups heavy cream

¼ cup (4 tbsp) unsalted butter

FOR THE GLAZE

⅔ cup plus 2 tbsp chopped 70% chocolate

½ cup heavy cream

1 tbsp golden syrup

1 tbsp unsalted butter, at room temperature

To make the cake, line a 9x13-inch pan with parchment paper, or fold a piece of parchment paper to this size, complete with sides and corners, and put on a baking sheet. Melt the chocolate, brown sugar and butter with the zest (in the microwave or over hot water). Stir in the salt. The mixture at this point will look as if something has gone wrong, but do not lose heart. Beat the eggs and the 2 tbsp sugar in a mixer or with an handheld electric mixer until pale and slightly thickened—about 5 minutes—and fold into the chocolate, followed by the flour and nuts. Put into the pan and spread evenly—it will be very thin. Bake at 325°F (275°F convection) for 10–15 minutes, till just firm (a skewer will emerge slightly sticky). Cool on a rack.

Make the mousse filling. Put the dark and milk chocolate in a bowl, ideally metal. Bring 1 cup of the cream to the boil and pour over, let stand for a minute and then stir till smooth. Chill until firm, about 2 hours.

When it is firm, put the metal bowl over a pan of just simmering water until partly melted, 3–5 minutes (do not stir). Remove from heat, add the butter and beat with an handheld electric mixer until thick and glossy, about 3 minutes. Beat the remaining ½ cup cream to soft peaks and fold into the filling. Put in the fridge while you deal with the cake.

TO DECORATE

thin slices of crystallized orange zest, extra toasted hazelnuts, chocolate curls or shards

You will need a board covered with foil, or a cake board, about 14x5-inches.

Chocolate curls take a bit of practice. You can make small curls with a potato peeler. For bigger curls use the biggest block of chocolate you can find. Get out a board and your largest knife. Microwave the chocolate in 30-second, then 10-second, bursts until it begins to soften ever so slightly—if it starts to go shiny or melt you have gone too far.

Put the chocolate on the board with one short end facing you, put a paper towel at the near end and pull into your midriff so that the chocolate cannot slide about. Use your largest knife (not serrated), holding the blunt top of the blade with one hand, the handle with the other. Now drag the blade towards you, scraping up curls. Put the curls into a plastic box and when you have enough, refrigerate. Save the block of chocolate for future curl-making.

Cut the cake lengthwise into two 13x4-inch strips. Put one on the serving board. Spread with about ½ cup of the mousse and put the other on top. To ensure the finished cake is a good shape, put the remaining mousse mixture into a piping bag with a large plain nozzle and pipe on top of the cake in long lines, using up all the mixture. Smooth with a spatula and chill for an hour, till firm.

For the glaze, put the chocolate in a bowl. Bring the cream and syrup to the boil and pour over the chocolate. Leave for 5 minutes then stir till smooth. Stir in butter till melted, then let stand till room temperature but still pourable, about 30 minutes. Spoon over the top of the chilled cake, using a spatula to smooth over the sides. Decorate with orange, nuts and chocolate curls, then leave to set, about 2 hours, or overnight.

You can customize the decoration as you wish—but whatever you do, be lavish. For Christmas or birthdays, add candles or sparklers.

Cut in small slices to serve—this cake is rich.

Gaillac doux is the sweet wine of our region; it is delicate and floral without being overpowering or syrupy. This understated dessert—no cooking required—does not need cream or ice cream to adorn it, though a dish of Walnut-Armagnac biscotti (page 236) adds an extra dimension.

Peaches in Gaillac Doux

Serves 6

half a bottle of Gaillac doux, or other sweet wine

4–5 ripe peaches or nectarines

a handful of raspberries, small strawberries or *fraises de bois*, to serve

Pour the wine into a large bowl and taste—add extra sugar, or a squeeze of lemon, to your taste.

Skin the peaches or nectarines by putting in a bowl, pouring over copious boiling water, waiting 15 seconds and checking to see if the skin of one of the peaches pulls away easily when nicked with a small knife. The moment this is the case, lift out with a slotted spoon and transfer a big bowl of cold water. Slide the skins off, then slice the peaches as attractively as you can straight into the wine. Mix gently, cover the surface with plastic wrap to keep the peaches submerged and chill for about an hour. Spoon into glasses and serve, scattered with a few berries. If you have a patch of *fraises de bois* in a shady part of the garden, this is the dessert to highlight them— just a few make a very pretty finish

RAYNAUDES SECRET

Peaches are at their finest in August. White peaches are much prized by the French but tend to go a little bit sand-colored when you peel them. My favorites are *pêches de vigne*— intensely dark peaches from the Burgundy area, reputedly planted at the ends of vine rows to signal disease, but now much prized for eating.

In 2006 the cherry crop from our orchard was so momentous that we collected over 220 pounds of fruit and had it distilled by Laurent Cazottes at Villeneuve-sur-Vère into exclusive Raynaudes cherry *eau de vie* (kirsch). This dish is intended to showcase the *eau de vie*, as well as being a delicious tasting plate of our desserts.

Deconstructed Black Forest Gateau

Serves 12

Chocolate nirvana (page 186)

Dark and deadly chocolate mousse (page 187)—half quantity

Vanilla ice cream (page 200)

Tuile mixture flavored with cocoa and shaped into small baskets (pages 231–33)

Chocolate curls (page 196)

kirsch or *eau de vie de cerises*, straight from the freezer

FOR THE CHERRIES

¼ cup plus 2 tbsp granulated sugar

⅔ cup red wine

60 fresh cherries, pitted

Cut the chilled Chocolate nirvana into 12 mini cakes using a small plain round cutter.

Spoon the mousse mixture into 12 miniature dishes and chill.

About an hour before serving, scoop the ice cream into the biscuit baskets and put back in the freezer.

For the cherries, bring the sugar and wine to the boil and boil hard to reduce to a thick syrup. Add the cherries and boil for 2 minutes, then leave to cool with a saucer on top so the cherries are completely submerged (or they will discolor). When cold, chill.

To assemble, first check the cherry syrup—if it has gone too thin, strain into a small pan and quickly boil it down till it is once more thick (this only takes 3–4 minutes). Set aside to cool.

On each of 12 large plates, put a mini-chocolate cake, a mousse, the ice cream (topped with a chocolate curl) and 5 cherries, topped with a little syrup. Add a shot glass of iced kirsch and serve.

You can make this esoteric but delectable dish if you have a black currant bush, and only in the month of May. You need to catch the plant a couple of weeks after it first comes into leaf—at which point the leaves are powerfully and sweetly aromatic.

Blackcurrant leaf sorbet

Serves 6–8

3–4 good handfuls of fresh young black currant leaves, washed

juice of 5 lemons

1 cup granulated sugar

2 tbsp vodka (optional)

Along with nasturtium butter (nasturtium petals stirred into softened butter, formed into a log and served in slices to accompany bread) and geranium marshmallows (I am not joking), this dish represents the offbeat side of the Raynaudes repertoire. The window for black currant leaf is extremely small, but by the same principles you can make a hauntingly delicious geranium sorbet all year round.

Bring 2 cups water to the boil and immerse the leaves in it. Leave to steep for about 10 minutes. Smell and taste. Strain the liquid, squeezing the leaves well, and discard the leaves. Stir in the lemon juice, sugar and a pinch of salt to dissolve and leave until completely cold. If using vodka, stir in at this point.

Either freeze in an ice-cream machine, or freeze in ice-cube trays, chop in batches in the food processor and refreeze. This latter method will give a texture some-where between a sorbet and a granita.

MAKE IT LOOK GREAT

If you grow your own red or white currants as well as black currants, freeze a few perfect sprigs as they ripen to use over the following winter and spring as a frosted decoration for this and other fruit desserts. Roll the frozen currants gently in a small bowl of sifted confectioners' sugar, and serve at once, to add a tart crunch.

My streamlined method for making ice cream uses the minimum of ingredients and equipment, and is so easy that we make it fresh practically every day in high summer.

Raynaudes vanilla ice cream

Makes 1 quart

1 cup whole milk

¾ cup sugar (granulated or Demerara)

6 egg yolks

about ¼ tsp cornstarch

about 2⅓ cups heavy cream, chilled

1 tsp vanilla extract

vanilla seeds from ½ pod (optional)

The Manoir kitchen is an intensely busy operation, and I do not believe in cutting corners. That said, the faster and more efficiently we can make something, the more time there is to make something extra—for instance, a new petit four with which to astonish guests after dinner this evening, or a pot of apricot jam for breakfast tomorrow.

I therefore make no apologies for my ultimately streamlined method for making ice cream. It not only contains the minimum of ingredients—it also uses precisely 6 pieces of equipment: measuring scales, measuring cup, mini whisk, microwave, ice-cream maker, freezer.

Put the measuring cup (which needs to be microwave-safe) on the scales. Put in the milk, weigh in the sugar, add the yolks and whisk in the cornstarch. Microwave at full power for 1 minute (for some reason, my whisk does not cause sparks, so it stays in the cup all the time). Whisk. Repeat this twice more. Now go to 30-second increments. After two or three 30-second bursts, the surface of the custard will begin to look a bit crusted. Stop and whisk vigorously. (There is no need to check, but out of interest, if you have a thermometer, it should read between 169°F and 180°F, which is the correct temperature for cooking custard.)

Stir in the cream to make 1 quarter, plus the vanilla. Chill this mixture thoroughly in your freezer—till almost frozen—then churn in an ice-cream maker.

Make Your Own Ice Cream

I have made ice creams freehand—without the use of an ice-cream maker—but with the honorable exception of granitas (grainy sorbets made from high-summer fruits such as nectarines and plums, and occasionally lemon), I prefer my ice cream whippy and deluxe. In 2007 we invested in a large Musso ice-cream machine, which almost noiselessly churns and freezes mixtures into unbelievably smooth and voluptuous ice creams. Kitchen gadgets and appliances are generally there to make the cook's life easier, but on this occasion the difference is the quality of the result. Since coming into ownership of the Bentley of ice-cream machines, we have made every conceivable flavor, in plain, rippled and chunked varieties. Here are my own golden rules.

- When making mixtures, be aware that the taste buds are blunted by chilled and frozen foods, and flavoring needs to be extra intense.

- It is a waste of time putting lukewarm—or even merely cold—mixtures into an ice cream machine. They will take ages to freeze. Far better to chill the mixture in the freezer section of your fridge for a couple of hours till just beginning to freeze, then transfer to the machine.

- If adding finishing touches such as fruit purée, nuts, chopped chocolate, to the mixture, fold in by hand when the ice cream is frozen as it is unlikely the machine will distribute it through the ice cream exactly how you wish it done.

- Homemade ice cream and sorbets do not keep well. They are at their best churned in the afternoon and eaten in the evening. After that the texture gets hard, and tempering—softening gently in the fridge—often means the outside part gets melted and the core remains rock solid. And the flavor is blunted. This is especially true of fruit sorbets.

- For me, all ice creams are taken into the Premier League by being topped with a swirl of whipped cream, made by whipping 1 cup cream with 1 tbsp sugar and 1 tsp vanilla extract (or our own vanilla bourbon, see page 192) till stiff. This can be piped or spooned on to the ice cream.

- Other finishing touches include a squeeze of coulis, a chocolate shard or curl (see page 196), caramelized nuts, chocolate raisins and frosted mint leaves (see page 188).

- If you are a perfectionist, ice cream can be tricky to serve as it, well, melts. To stop it sliding around on its way to the table, leaving a sticky trail across the plate, we put it in a discreet tuile cup. To make these, bake small tuile biscuits (see pages 231–33) and while still hot mold them into small dishes or ramekins.

This has become a well-known recipe, but I searched for many months to find a practical version that can be got ready well ahead and popped in the oven at the last moment. You can make the fondants up to 8 hours in advance: refrigerate, lightly covered in plastic wrap, then remove half an hour before baking.

Chocolate fondant

Makes 8

melted butter and granulated sugar, to prepare the ramekins

1 stick (8 tbsp) unsalted butter

1¾ cups dark plain chocolate, coarsely chopped

4 large eggs plus one yolk

1 tsp vanilla extract

½ cup plus 1 tbsp superfine sugar

2 level tbsp all-purpose flour

You will need eight ¼-cup ramekins

Prepare the ramekins by brushing with melted butter and dusting with granulated sugar. If you are of a nervous disposition, cut out little discs of parchment paper and put in the bottom, though they are not necessary.

Melt the butter with the chocolate (in the microwave, or see page 211). In an electric mixer, whisk the eggs, yolk, vanilla, sugar and ¼ tsp salt for 5 minutes. The eggs should be moussey and leave a temporary trail when you remove the whisk. Scrape the melted chocolate over the top, then sprinkle over the flour. Now fold all together gently but thoroughly till the mixture is a no longer streaked. Pour into ramekins. (Sometimes for added ooziness I press a frozen chocolate truffle into the middle of each fondant just before baking.)

Bake for 13–15 minutes at 400°F (375°F convection). They are ready when they have a thin firm crust on top but the centers jiggle slightly when gently shaken; the centers should still be liquid. Remove from oven. Run a small knife round the edge of the ramekin and invert onto serving plate. Leave the ramekin in place and continue with other fondants. When all are inverted, remove the ramekins, dust the fondants with cocoa powder or confectioners' sugar if you wish and serve with whipped cream or ice cream.

Make it look great

This is a sensory treat served with ice cream. I bake tiny chocolate baskets from the tuile mixture mixed with a little cocoa (see pages 231–33), and about half an hour before serving fill with a scoop of fresh mint ice cream. This waits in the freezer till the exciting moment of serving arrives.

Fresh mint ice cream

Follow the recipe on page 200, but flavor the milk by heating it to boiling with a good handful of young mint sprigs. Leave covered for half an hour, then strain and continue with the recipe, omitting the vanilla.

In the autumn I have to bring our twelve small lemon trees into the greenhouse. This commotion is repaid by the delicious scent of the lemon blossom in late winter and a modest crop of lemons. I refuse to use these for general cooking—instead they are used for tea, or this refreshing Italian liqueur.

Limoncello

Makes two 750ml bottles

5 lemons, fresh as you can get (you will not need juice for this recipe)

4¼ cups grappa, vodka or alcohol for fruits

1 cup granulated sugar

Scrub the lemons and soak overnight in cold water. (If you grow your own lemons, they come in all sizes, so this is a good recipe to use up the little ones—you will of course need to scale up the number.) Drain and dry. Remove the zest with a zester, sharp knife, potato peeler or grater.

Now you have a choice. Either put the zest into a large bottle or jar and add the grappa. Or use a funnel and feed the lemon zest through it into the bottle of grappa. Seal, shake well and leave for a month, stirring occasionally.

Dissolve the sugar in 1¼ cups water, then boil for a minute and leave to cool. Mix this syrup with the lemon-grappa mixture, shake well, then strain into clean bottles. If you are an amateur winemaker you may have special filters to clarify drinks, otherwise the liqueur will settle into a clear yellow liquid and a milky sediment, which should be shaken before serving to make a slightly opaque drink.

MAKE IT LOOK GREAT

Keep this in the freezer, which will slightly thicken the liqueur. Serve in tiny shot glasses.

RAYNAUDES SECRET

In France every supermarket and off license sells neat alcohol for making liqueurs and bottling fruits. If you live in Britain, it is worth seeking out to take home, as are bottles of pure cane sugar syrup (*pur sirop de canne*) for cocktails.

These are after-dinner brownies for adults, rich, dense and sweet. Beating the eggs to a mousse is what gives the lush texture and sugary crust. We cut the brownies into tiny triangles and serve as petits fours (shown on page 208).

After-Dinner brownies

Makes an 8-inch square, cutting into about 50 tiny brownies

1 stick (8 tbsp) plus 5 tbsp unsalted butter

10 ounces 70% chocolate, of which all but about 3½ ounces broken up, the remainder in small squares

⅔ cup all-purpose flour

½ cup cocoa

3 large eggs

1¼ cups plus 2 tbsp superfine sugar

cocoa, for dusting (optional)

You will need an 8-inch square brownie pan, or baking pan lined with a double thickness of foil (make overhangs generous so you can lift the brownies out, when baked and cooled, using the foil as handles)

Melt the butter with the 1 cup plus 6 tbsp chocolate in a bowl, either over hot water or in the microwave (about 2 minutes on high).

Sift the flour, cocoa and a pinch of salt into a bowl (keep the sieve to hand).

Whisk the eggs and sugar together, using an electric stand mixer or handheld mixer, for 3–8 minutes (depending on how powerful your mixer is) until thick and foamy. When you lift out the beaters, the egg should leave a short-lived trail on the surface of the egg rather than sink straight into it.

Pour the chocolate mixture over the surface of the egg mixture, then gently fold in with a large spatula until evenly mixed. Now sift over the flour-cocoa mixture and start to fold this in. Before it is fully amalgamated, tip in the chopped chocolate and continue folding, stopping just before the flour is fully mixed (you should spot some flecks of unmixed flour—trust me, this is correct).

Bake at 350°F (325°F convection) for 22–30 minutes until the cake no longer wobbles in the middle and the sides are just beginning to come away from the tin. A toothpick or skewer inserted into the center of the cake should emerge with sticky crumbs attached (unless you accidentally speared a piece of chocolate, in which case try again). Brownies are better underbaked than overbaked.

Remove from pan when cold and peel off foil, if using. Cut into desired shapes. The brownies should have a sugary, almost papery crust, which looks attractive in itself (though it will be much shattered by the time you have cut them) but you can, if you wish, dust them with a little cocoa.

MAKE IT LOOK GREAT

For an impromptu birthday celebration you can stick birthday candles into a few of these triangles—though if you do, be sure not to dust them with cocoa or you will end up with a cocoa snowstorm when they are blown out.

This is probably our most popular truffle. The inclusion of fresh herbs means guests can almost persuade themselves it is a healthy option.

Fresh mint truffles

Makes 20–30 truffles—these keep for a week in the fridge

1¼ cup heavy cream

six 6-inch sprigs of fresh mint

1 pound 70% chocolate

cocoa

Bring the cream to the boil in a small pan with a lid. Stir in the mint, making sure it is fully submerged, and leave to steep, covered, for half an hour. Strain into a 2-cup measure, pressing down firmly on the mint—you need 1¼ cup flavored cream (top up if necessary). Bring back to the boil.

Break the chocolate up into the processor bowl and whiz to chop. Pour over the boiling cream, wait for 1 minute, then process till smooth. Transfer to a metal bowl and chill. (When chilling mixtures quickly—for ice cream or chocolates, for instance—a metal bowl speeds up the process and gives you more control over temperature.)

When firm, spoon teaspoon-size balls of the mixture on to a foil-lined baking sheet. Roll them quickly between your palms, drop into cocoa then put them back on the baking sheet and chill thoroughly. If the mixture seems to be getting soft and sticky at any point, re-chill.

MAKE IT LOOK GREAT

Fresh truffles look Jacobean-dapper in little white paper cases, or you can wrap them in squares of colored foil.

Flavored truffles: mint is just one of those that we serve at the Manoir—other favorites being violet (in honor of our local city, Toulouse), espresso (flavored with an intense coffee extract made by Trablit) and passionfruit. Each requires a different formula, but fresh fruit truffles are the most tricky to make, being so soft that they have to be enrobed in chocolate before dipping in cocoa—or you would never get them from plate to mouth. This is such a messy process that you can guarantee the phone will ring or a guest arrive in the middle of it.

Clockwise from top left: Vanilla marshmallows, Macarons au chocolat, After-dinner brownies, Millionaire mendiants, Cocoa-nib florentines and Fresh mint truffles; and down the center, in the two square dishes: chocolate-covered raisins soaked in Sauternes (a store-bought local speciality) and Choc-walnut-Armagnac fudge.

The requirement for an after-dinner chocolate or petit four at Raynaudes is that it be intense, exciting—and just one mouthful. This is all those things, as well as being relatively quick and easy to make. It keeps in the fridge for a couple of weeks, or you can freeze it.

Choc-walnut-Armagnac fudge

Makes about 50 miniscule rectangles

3¾ cups plus 1 tbsp dark chocolate (about 70% cocoa solids), chopped

½ tsp baking soda

one 14-ounce can sweetened condensed milk

1 tbsp vanilla extract

3–4 tbsp Armagnac

1 cup walnuts, toasted and roughly chopped

You will need an 8-inch square pan lined with foil and very lightly greased

Mix the chocolate in a bowl with the baking soda, then stir in the condensed milk, vanilla, 3 tbsp Armagnac and a pinch of salt. Put the bowl over a pan of just simmering water and stir constantly for 2–4 minutes until the chocolate is almost fully melted (but not completely). Remove from heat and continue to stir for another 2–4 minutes until thick, smooth and glossy. If after this time the mixture looks like it is seizing or splitting, add more Armagnac, teaspoon by teaspoon, until it has homogenized. Stir in the walnuts and pour into the pan. Refrigerate and when completely set, cut into squares.

Cooking with Chocolate

There are more myths around cooking with chocolate than virtually any other branch of cookery. Most problems occur when, horrifyingly, your glossy melted chocolate turns into a tarry scrambled mess. The most common misconception is that "seizing" is caused by overheating the chocolate. It is far more likely to be caused by incorrect addition of liquid to chocolate. And this may not be your fault—or even the recipe writer's fault—as different chocolates can behave differently.

If—like most cooks—you have thrown away batches of curdled chocolate in despair, here is what you need to know.

- Chocolate can be melted by itself (or with a fat such as butter), over just simmering water (the bain-marie technique) or in the microwave (stirring every 30 seconds). Use whichever method you prefer, but if using a bain-marie, be aware that no water must come into contact with the chocolate—danger points being because your bowl was wet to begin with, your spoon is wet, or water spills in from the pan below. Whether microwaving or using a bain-marie, removing the chocolate before it is fully liquid and leaving it to finish melting away from the heat will rule out any possibility of overheating.

- Chocolate can be melted in the same way with other liquids (cream, brandy, even water) as long as there is enough liquid. Enough means about 1 tablespoon liquid to 1¾ ounces chocolate. If you do not have enough liquid, the chocolate will seize. If the recipe you are following does not appear to involve the right amount of liquid—you have been warned.

- In the event chocolate has for whatever reason seized, do not blindly soldier on—you need to rectify the problem before continuing. But this is not impossible. The trick is to stir in more liquid, teaspoon by teaspoon, until the chocolate is thick and glossy once more. To avoid throwing the balance of the recipe, use some of the liquid from elsewhere in the method (for instance, a few spoonfuls of beaten egg, or some cream from later on). Failing that, add water and accept that your finished dish may be a little less firmly set, or need a little longer in the oven, than stipulated in the recipe.

I have used certain chocolates with very high (for instance 85%) cocoa solids that have seized at the shake of a stick. Though I have always been able to bring them back by adding extra liquid, I rarely have problems with 70 or 72% cocoa solids, so now I stick to those for cooking.

Mendiants are popular throughout southern France. At the Manoir they are practically papal—being adorned with sprinkles of crystallized flower petals, chunks of crystallized fruits and even scraps of gold leaf.

Millionaire mendiants

Makes 20–30

7 ounces of your favorite dark chocolate

TO DECORATE

toasted hazelnuts, raisins, crystallized flowers such as violet and rose, crystallized orange peel, edible gold leaf

The story behind mendiants is as complicated as anything you will find in *The Da Vinci Code*. Originally *Les Mendiants* was the name for a Christmas treat consisting of a dish of almonds, figs, hazelnuts and raisins—whose colors are those of the four Roman Catholic mendicant orders (Dominicans—white, Franciscans,—gray, Carmelites—brown, Augustinians—deep purple). Later these dried fruits and nuts became stuck on to little coins of chocolate.

Prepare your decorations and lay them out on the work surface. Line a baking sheet with foil. Melt the chocolate—temper it if you are a perfectionist (see below)—and put small spoonfuls on to the foil. Immediately decorate with the fruits and nuts. Put in the fridge to set. Do not try to make dozens at once—although they keep very well, the chocolate will begin to set before you have stuck on the fruit and nuts.

MAKE IT LOOK GREAT

For pop-art mendiants, melt a little white chocolate and add drops to the discs of chocolate after you have put them on the foil but before decoration. Quickly swirl the white chocolate with a toothpick, then add your fruit and nuts. Groovy!

For more understated mendiants, pound a little saffron and stir into the chocolate when melted. Spoon into discs and decorate with just a scrap of gold leaf.

RAYNAUDES SECRET

Tempering results in crisp, gleaming, professional-looking chocolates. Without tempering, if you simply melt the chocolate and let it set, your mendiants will taste marvelous and look pretty—but the chocolate will have a dull, almost matte finish. I have tried various methods, but the only one that works for me involves a thermometer and a powdered cocoa-solid product made by Barry-Cailebaut called Mycryo. You melt the chocolate to about 100°F, cool it to 93–95°F and sift in 1% of Mycryo (so for 7 ounces of chocolate, ⅛ ounce Mycryo). When the chocolate cools to 88°F it is ready to use.

I celebrated my fortieth birthday in New York, and a friend threw a party of people she thought I would like to meet. One of them was one of the greatest of American cookery writers, Dorie Greenspan, on whose recipe (in collaboration with Pierre Hermé in *Chocolate Desserts*) this is based.

Macarons au chocolat

Makes about 48 tiny macaroons for petits fours

½ cup blanched almonds

1¼ cups confectioners' sugar

2½ tbsp cocoa

1¼ oz egg whites (about 1 egg white—beating will help you measure)

FOR THE GANACHE

¾ cup chopped 70% chocolate

⅔ cup heavy cream

knob of butter at room temperature

Process the almonds with the confectioners' sugar and cocoa as fine as possible. Beat the egg whites till stiff, then fold in the dry ingredients in three or four goes. The result should be rather wet and sloppy. Transfer to a piping bag with a round nozzle and pipe small dollops (about 1 inch wide) on to a baking sheet lined with baking paper. (Dorie's tip—put a tiny dollop of mixture on each corner of the parchment sheet to stop the baking paper sliding round.) Bang the sheet firmly down on the counter to remove air bubbles, leave for 15 minutes, dust with a little cocoa and bake for 8–10 minutes at 425°F (400°F convection). Repeat with remaining mixture.

For the ganache, put the chocolate pieces in a bowl. Bring the cream to a rolling boil, pour over the chocolate, leave for 5 minutes without stirring, then stir together till smooth. Add the butter and stir again till smooth. Chill.

This sounds odd, but to release the macaroons from the paper, run a little cold water carefully between the paper and the baking sheet beneath. Just this hint of moisture is enough to make them slip off, though obviously you do not want the water to come on top of the paper and wet the macaroons. Sandwich the macaroons with a tiny ball of chocolate ganache, rolled between your palms.

Fashionable cocoa nibs—small ground pieces of cocoa bean—give a deep, nutty, slightly bitter flavor to these very grown-up after-dinner cookies, which are a cross between a tuile and a florentine.

Cocoa-nib florentines

Makes about 30

3½ tbsp unsalted butter

¼ cup heavy cream

⅓ cup plus 1 tbsp granulated sugar

2½ tbsp all-purpose flour

1½ ounces shelled pistachios, toasted and chopped

1½ ounces cocoa nibs

3½ ounces 70% chocolate, melted, to finish

You will need a rolling pin or tuile mold

Line 2 baking sheets with parchment paper (or a nonstick silicone mat). You will need to bake the cookies in 2 batches (i.e. 4 sheets' worth), because they spread.

Melt the butter and add all other ingredients except the melted chocolate. Cook, stirring all the time, for about 3 minutes, until the mixture thickens slightly and starts to come away from the sides of the pan. Remove from the heat.

Put scant teaspoonfuls (otherwise they will come out enormous) on to the lined baking sheets, allowing plenty of room for spreading. Bake at 350°F (same temperature for convection open) for 10–12 minutes, until just beginning to turn color. Let them cool for half a minute, then when they are just firm enough to handle, use a palette knife to drape them into the tuile mold or over a rolling pin, to give a curved shape. Repeat until all the batter is used.

Leave the cookies to cool completely. If you have time, leave the coating to the following day, as the cookies will be less fragile. To coat, simply paint the melted chocolate on to the convex side and put on a foil-lined baking sheet to set.

You have never really tasted a marshmallow until you have made your own. Superlight and fragrant with vanilla, you may never again want to eat one of those squashed mini tennis balls out of a bag.

Homemade vanilla marshmallows

Makes about 20 medium-size marshmallows

scant ½ cup granulated sugar

3 gelatine leaves

2 ounces egg white (about 1½ egg whites—whisking will help you measure)

1 tsp vanilla extract

confectioners' sugar, for dusting

You will need a rectangular baking pan, about 8x10-inches, or a square equivalent

Line the baking pan with plastic wrap—easier if you wet the pan slightly first. Next measure the sugar into a small pan with ⅓ cup water. Put the gelatine leaves next to a bowl of cold water. Put the egg whites into the bowl of a electric mixer, with the vanilla and a measuring spoon to hand.

You now need to do several things at the same time. Bring the sugar and water to the boil, stirring to dissolve, then set a timer for 6 minutes. Put the gelatine leaves in the water to soak. Start whisking the egg whites at a slow speed and continue till stiff peaks form. At 6 minutes check the sugar syrup—it should be slightly thickened (if not continue for a minute or two longer).

Remove the gelatine from the water, squeeze lightly with your hand and put into the syrup, which you have removed from the heat.

Now with the mixer running on high speed, add the syrup to the egg whites in a thin stream. Once it is all in, continue whipping for 5 full minutes, until the mixture is stiff and shiny. Add the vanilla 1 minute before the end. Transfer to the lined pan, smoothing the top with a spatula, and let set at room temperature for 3 hours.

Cut in squares and dip immediately in confectioners' sugar to coat. The marshmallows will keep for a day or two.

You can vary the flavor by adding 1 tbsp rose water or geranium water (available from some Middle-Eastern shops), for instance, and some drops of coloring.

Baking, Tea and Breakfast

The Raynaudes "wood-fired oven" LOAF

Walnut ROLLS

Dinner ROLLS

Cheese *and* chilli BREAD

Comté SCONES

Pine nut *and* rosemary COOKIES

Toasted almond TUILES

Forgotten COOKIES

Walnut-Armagnac BISCOTTI

Homemade digestives

Raynaudes pain perdu

Tropical banana CAKE

Fresh apricot JAM

Homemade vanilla YOGURT

Honey almond granola

The Raynaudes smoothie

I dream of having my own wood-fired oven to cook in, but in the meantime I have found a way to bake a loaf of bread with a fabulous crust. The dough itself is very simple.

The Raynaudes "wood fired oven" loaf

Makes 1 loaf

walnut-size piece fresh yeast (see overleaf)

1¼ cups lukewarm water

1 pound bread flour

1½ tsp salt

a little cornmeal

You will need a very large oval or round Le Creuset-type casserole with lid (mine is 15x12-inches, and 6 inches deep)

Dissolve the yeast in the water. Put the flour and salt in the processor, turn on and add the yeast mixture through the feed tube. Once the mixture has combined, count to 45 then stop. Use your hands to scoop the mixture out and knead for about 30 seconds by hand. (I make this in our heavy-duty Robot Coupe food processor, although any large strong processor should do the job. Otherwise, mix the ingredients in a food processor fitted with the dough hook and knead for 5 minutes, or mix them in a bowl, transfer to work surface and knead by hand for 10 minutes before continuing with the next step.)

Put the dough in a greased bowl, covered with plastic wrap. Leave in a warm place to double in size—1–2 hours. Turn gently out on to a floured work top and pat out into a rectangle about 9x12-inches. Roll up from the longer side and shape with floured hands into a small rugby-ball shape with seam underneath (if the casserole in which you will be baking is oval) or football (if the casserole is round). Cut a piece of parchment paper to about 1½ times the length or diameter of the casserole and sprinkle lightly with cornmeal. Put the loaf on it, cover loosely with a light tea towel or greased plastic wrap and leave to rise till about 1½ times its original size, 45 minutes to an hour.

At the start of this final rising, put the casserole with lid into the oven and turn it to 450°F (use conventional oven setting to bake this loaf rather than convection setting).

Getting the risen loaf into the oven needs to be done quickly and smoothly, so walk it through before you proceed. Score 3 or 4 shallow slashes on the top of the

loaf with a sharp blade. Lift the casserole out of the oven on to a heat-proof surface and set the lid alongside. Holding the ends of the parchment paper, lift the bread and carefully lower it into the hot casserole, paper and all. Put on the lid and place in the oven for 30 minutes. At this point, remove the lid—the bread will already be golden and crusty—and bake uncovered until fully cooked, about 10 minutes longer.

Remove to a rack—the crust should crack and craze as it cools—and leave until completely cold before eating.

You can double this recipe, but if you do, leave one of the loaves to make its second rising in a cool place, or give it its first half hour rising in the fridge, to slow it down so you can cook it after the first has come out. If you have 3 ½ ounces or so of cooked mashed potato to hand, you can add it to the bread with the flour to give a more savory flavor and rich, coppery color.

Make your own bread

France taking such a pride in its artisan bakery tradition, many guests are surprised that we have never served a loaf of bought bread at the Manoir. This is partly because one of the privileges of running a table d'hôtes with a set menu is that you can choose what you cook every day, so I have made literally hundreds of different batches of breads using dozens of different recipes, techniques and formulas, exactly to my requirements on the day. It's also because our nearest artisan baker is a 14 mile round trip away.

Countless books have been written about bread making, but here is my personal take on this fascinating subject.

- Fresh yeast is more reliable and works faster than dried. If translating a recipe from one to the other, I use twice the weight of fresh to dried, regardless of whether the recipe specifies instant, traditional or easy-blend dried yeast. Having said this, the yeast is only one of several variables in bread making, and quantity is not as critical as, say, the amount of baking powder in a cake. If you use too little yeast, the bread may be slower to rise but it will usually get there in the end.

- By preference, I mix the dough in my food mixer (usually 5 minutes with the dough hook) or heavy-duty food processor (45 seconds from the dough coming together in the processor bowl). If your processor stalls or cannot handle this amount of dough, you can process it in 2 batches—no need to wash the bowl up after emptying out the first. I usually then give the dough a short (30-second or 1-minute) hand-knead before its first rise.

- The wetter your dough, the more tender and flavorsome your bread. Do not be frightened of using plenty of flour on your hands and work top when trying to handle wet doughs. A dough that is unmanageably sticky when it comes out of the mixer will usually become manageable after the first rise, as long as you use plenty of flour to help you.

- You can retard the first or second rise from 1 hour to about 5 hours by putting the dough in the fridge. You can bake the risen dough directly from the fridge, or bring it out half an hour before baking. This is very convenient if you want to make the dough in the morning and cook the bread before dinner (specially rolls, which are best eaten very fresh).

- I am very gentle when knocking back. I gently deflate it by pressing, rather than punching, then fold or roll it prior to shaping. I never re-knead at this point as I find it makes the finished bread tough and dense.

- You can improve the crust on loaves by misting before baking and a couple more times during the first 5 minutes of baking (do not worry about opening the oven door to do this, it will not spoil the bread). You can also bake the bread within a large cast-iron casserole (as on page 218) or on a baking tile set at the bottom of the oven (see page 112).

- Rolls are best served warm from the oven, loaves best allowed to cool fully.

- Loaves are like tapestries, they tell a story. No two, even from the same batch, are identical; each one is subtly different depending on how it was mixed and handled. Over time you develop a sixth sense for how your dough is behaving, but never try and make bread against the clock, and don't rush the shaping stage, so your bread looks as beautiful as it tastes.

- A note on sourdough. Over three years I have a developed a sourdough culture that we use to make our own sourdough bread. It is a combination of three cultures—one developed in the Raynaudes kitchen from organic grapes, and two sent as gifts by American visitors. Many books explain the art of making sourdough bread in depth, but I have discovered that your starter will have much more bounce and energy if you feed it generously. When feeding my starter, I use a formula of 1 cup starter, 1 cup water and 1⅔ cups flour (most recipes suggest ½ cup plus 2 tbsp flour). During the summer I put the culture to sleep in the freezer (once removed and fed twice a day, it takes three days to full recovery). Sourdough bread freezes very well so I make loaves every day for a month in April to keep us supplied till midsummer.

I have tried many different recipes for walnut bread. The nuttiest of all—inspired by the walnut bread made by fashionable French baker Poilâne—uses an amazing half pound walnuts to 4 cups flour, and is so dense it seems more nut than bread. These rolls, made on the Chelsea bun principle, are lighter and fun to make.

Walnut rolls

dribble of honey (about ½ tsp)

1⅛ cups warm water

walnut-size piece fresh yeast
(see page 220)

2½ cups bread flour

1⅓ cups whole wheat flour

3–5 tbsp olive oil, walnut oil or
a mixture

FOR THE FILLING

1¼ cups walnuts, lightly toasted
and roughly chopped

2 shallots, finely chopped and
lightly browned

3 tbsp chopped herbs, such as
parsley, thyme or rosemary

3 tbsp olive oil, plus a little
extra

*You will need a roasting pan or
deep baking pan about 10x13-
inches, oiled*

You can use this same technique (which I learned from Thane Prince at the Aldeburgh Cookery School) for other flavorings, such as caramelized onions, or cheese and herbs. Whatever you choose, be very generous with the filling.

Make the dough in the processor. Put the honey in a measuring cup with the water. Whisk in the yeast. Put the flours in the processor bowl with 1 tsp salt and add the liquid and oil through the feed tube with the machine running. Count to 45, turn out the dough and finish the kneading by hand for 1 minute. Leave to rise in a lightly oiled bowl covered with oiled plastic wrap for about 1–1½ hours till doubled in size.

Turn out on to a well-floured surface. If the dough is sticky, do not be alarmed, just use more flour. Roll out to a rectangle about 10x12-inches, with the long side parallel to the work surface. Fold the top third down, then the lower third up over it (just like folding a business letter). Turn round and roll out once again, using more flour, to as large a rectangle as you can comfortably manage—about 16x20-inches is ideal.

Sprinkle with nuts, shallots and herbs, then drizzle over a little oil. Roll up tightly from one of the long sides to make a long roll. Cut the roll into equal halves. Mark each one with your knife or dough scraper into 12 equal lengths (total of 24) then cut off one by one and lay cut-side down in the oiled tin. Arrange so you have 4 along the shorter side and 6 down the longer side, then fill in with the rest (see previous page).

Drizzle with a little more oil, cover again with the oiled clingfilm and leave to rise for 45 minutes to an hour, till risen to about half as big again. Bake at 400°F (350°F convection) for 25–30 minutes, till pale golden. Do not overbake this bread—it is done when the rolls are still tender and tinged with gold rather than crisp. Leave to cool for 10 minutes, turn out on to a cloth on a rack, then turn right-side up to cool on a rack.

Make it look great

We serve these rolls as one large bread on a breadboard and pass around for guests to tear them off.

Buying Flour in France

If you live in France and would like to experiment with breadmaking, here is what I have found out by trial and error.

- The local baker will usually sell you bread dough to take home and cook yourself—great for pizzas for a party. You can also buy frozen dough in supermarkets or frozen-food chain Picard.

- You can buy fresh yeast (*levure de boulangerie*) in small blocks in the refrigerator section of supermarkets. You can buy dried yeast near the flour—*traditionelle* is ordinary (dissolve in water), super is fast action (mix into flour).

- Flour (*farine*) is categorized by type. White comes in type 45 (superfine) and type 55 (ordinary). *Complète* is whole wheat; *seigle* is rye; *sarrasin* is buckwheat; *épeautre* is spelt; *farine à gateaux* is self-raising; *farine fluide* is sponge or cake flour, and *Maizena*, or *farine de maïs*, is cornstarch.

- You can buy special flour for bread (*farine à pain*) and many bread mixes in French supermarkets. If you look at their long lists of ingredients, however, they include flavor enhancers and deactivated yeast, presumably to make one's bread taste more bready.

- Owing to climate and varieties grown, French flour is traditionally weak. Indeed many of the French bread making traditions—very long proving times, tough

crusts with web-like crumb—are a response to the weakness of the flour. Type 45 and type 55 do not refer to flour strength. Look instead for the protein content, which is sometimes indicated on the label—for bread you require 10–12 percent protein.

- Finally, after many experiments (including adding extra gluten in powder form to increase elasticity), my local baker directed me to an excellent, fine, strong flour, *gruau*, which gives me the structure and elasticity I am looking for when making yeast breads.

The Raynaudes "wood-fired oven" loaf (see pages 218–9).

I love the moment at the beginning of a meal when bread is passed round among guests. If we are serving rolls, I sometimes bake them so they are lightly joined together, so that guests can break one off in a symbolic gesture of sharing.

Dinner rolls

Makes 24–30, depending on size

walnut-size piece fresh yeast

1¼ cups milk, warm (ideally boiled, cooled and skimmed)

2 tbsp granulated sugar

1 large egg

4 cups flour: half all-purpose, half bread flour

1 stick (8 tbsp) unsalted butter, softened

Mix the yeast, milk and sugar then beat in the egg. Put the flours and 1½ tsp salt in mixer bowl and beat in the milk mixture with the machine running for 1 minute, then the butter. Switch to the dough hook and knead for 4 minutes. Leave to rise till doubled in size—up to 2 hours.

Line 2 baking sheets with parchment paper. Punch the dough down lightly, leave it for 5 minutes to recover then turn on to lightly floured work surface. Shape into a 9-inch square, then fold in 3 like a letter. Use your hands with a backward and forward rolling motion to shape the dough into a 18-inch cylinder.

To make round rolls, cut off and weigh pieces of dough of 1½ ounces, then roll each one into a neat ball and place on the baking sheets.

Triangular rolls (which are called in Yorkshire, I am told, skufflers) are made by first shaping the dough into a very long, thin cylinder: roll the dough as above, but keep going patiently until you have a yard-long cylinder. Starting at one end, and alternating the knife 45 degrees to left and right, cut the sausage into 1½-inch triangles—you should have about 24. Place on baking sheets.

Whatever shape you have chosen, leave to rise covered by a light tea towel for 45 minutes to an hour. Bake at 375°F (350°F convection) oven for 15 minutes, till pale gold, switching sheets after 7 minutes so they cook evenly.

Chillies are great fun to grow but you end up with far more than you can possibly use. This bread does not really solve the problem, but it is fun to serve dotted with specks of different-colored homegrown chillies.

Cheese and chilli bread

Makes 1 large loaf

walnut-size piece fresh yeast

1¾ cups warm water

4½ cups bread flour

¼ cup olive oil

3 tbsp finely chopped deseeded chillies

¼ cup grated Comté or Cheddar cheese

generous ⅓ cup finely grated Parmesan

large egg, beaten with a pinch of salt, to glaze

You will need a 9x5-inch loaf pan, greased

Mix the yeast into the water in your mixer bowl and add the flour, 1½ tsp salt and the olive oil. Start mixing slowly, using the dough hook attachment, then knead for about 5 minutes, adding the chillies, three-quarters of the Comté and half of the Parmesan halfway through. Transfer to a large bowl (or leave in the mixer bowl), cover and leave to rise at room temperature. Because the added ingredients slow up the rising process, allow 2–2½ hours to double in size.

Turn out on to a floured surface (dough will be wet) and pat into a rectangle about 11x18-inches. With the 8-inch side facing you, fold in 3 like a letter, then transfer to the pan seam-side down. Leave to rise loosely covered in oiled plastic wrap until the bread comes above the top of the pan. Brush lightly with egg glaze (you will not need it all), then sprinkle with remaining cheese and bake at 400°F (350°F convection) for 40–50 minutes, until dark golden and hollow sounding. When the bread is done, put it upside down on a baking sheet (doesn't matter if it sits lopsidedly) and put back in the switched-off oven for 10 minutes to crisp the crust. Allow to cool fully before cutting.

Really quick and easy to make, crunchy on the outside and tender within. Comté is France's favorite and most readily available cheese, but you can use any strong hard cheese you fancy.

Comté scones

Makes 12–16

2¼ cups all-purpose flour

1 tbsp baking powder

2 tsp sugar

7 tbsp butter, cut into cubes

1¼ cups Comté or other strong hard cheese, grated

¾ cup heavy cream

1 large egg

Put the flour, baking powder, sugar and ½ tsp salt in the processor and whiz to blend. Add the butter and blend till very crumbly, then add the cheese and whiz briefly. Mix the cream and egg and then, with the machine running, add through the feed tube until the mixture just comes together—stop the machine immediately.

Without kneading or manhandling the dough, turn out on to a lightly floured surface, bring it together and divide in 2. Pat into 2 rounds of 8-inch diameter, then cut each into 6 or 8 wedges using a knife or scraper. Set on 2 ungreased baking sheets, well spaced, and bake for about 20 minutes at 375°F (350°F convection), till golden and cooked in the center (test with a skewer if in doubt).

Leave to cool on a rack and serve at room temperature or warm with butter.

These bite-size cookies are unusual and sophisticated. One guest asked for the recipe because she said she wanted to try and wean her grandchildren on to proper, grown-up cookies.

Pine nut and rosemary cookies

Makes about 3 dozen

2 tbsp pine nuts, toasted, plus 3 dozen extra for topping each cookie

2 tsp finely chopped fresh rosemary

1⅓ cups all-purpose flour

½ tsp baking soda

¼ tsp ground ginger

5 tbsp unsalted butter, softened

½ cup plus 2 tbsp superfine sugar

1 tbsp extra virgin olive oil

1½ tbsp heavy cream

1 egg yolk

Toast the pine nuts: the easiest way is in a dry frying pan over medium-high heat, shaking the pan constantly. Pulse the rosemary and toasted pine nuts in a processor till ground. Transfer to a bowl and add the flour, baking soda, ginger and a pinch of salt.

Cream the butter and sugar until pale and fluffy, either by hand or in a mixer, and add the oil. Mix in the flour, then the cream, then the egg yolk.

Shape into small balls just under ¼-inch in diameter and put 5cm apart on baking sheets lined with parchment paper (they flatten as they bake). Sprinkle with a little extra superfine sugar.

Bake at 325°F (same temperature for convection) for about 13 minutes, till the edges are golden. Top each one with a pine nut, let cool on sheet, then transfer to racks to cool further. (When baking cookies, unless I need the sheets for another batch, I often disobey a golden rule of baking and leave them to cool on the sheet itself, as here. Once cooled, they can be transferred directly to the box or storage container.)

This is a wonderful crunchy tuile cookie, tasting richly of toasted almonds and browned butter.

Toasted almond tuiles

Makes about 18

1 tbsp salted butter

⅓ cup superfine sugar

⅔ cup sliced almonds

2 tbsp all-purpose flour

2 ounces egg white (about 1½ egg whites—whisking will help you to measure)

You will need a rolling pin or tuile mold

Put the butter in a pan and, watching carefully, cook till pale brown, nutty and fragrant. Pour into a bowl and then add all remaining ingredients (which you have previously measured out) and a good pinch of salt. Stir well—it will look sticky and unpromising.

Heat the oven to 400°F (375°F convection). Line 2 baking sheets with parchment paper (I use nonstick silicone mat) and put the mixture in well-spaced teaspoonfuls on the paper, about 9 per sheet. Use a fork dipped in water to spread each teaspoon of the mixture out into a round shape about 2 inches in diameter (it will not spread or flatten much in the oven, so get the nuts evenly distributed at this point). Put the first baking sheet in the oven while you prepare the second.

Bake one sheet at a time for 5–6 minutes, removing each tuile when it is pale gold all over and lightly speckled (returning the rest on their tray to the oven) and laying on a rolling pin or in the mold before it hardens. Continue till all are cooked and shaped.

Tuiles and Shaped Cookies

Tuiles and shaped cookies are an important part of the chef's repertoire—useful to provide a texture contrast to creamy desserts, as a neat way to present ice cream, or as a visual highlight, if you go for crazy shapes.

BATTER

The recipe for almond tuiles on page 231 gives a crisp nutty cookie. When you are looking for something less assertive, I make up a batter by whisking ¼ cup plus 2 tbsp sugar with 3 egg whites till slightly foamy, then whisking in 1 stick (8 tbsp) melted butter, then ½ cup all-purpose flour and 1 tsp vanilla extract. This batter can be refrigerated for up to a week—bake the cookies as you need them. It is baked at a lower temperature than the almond—350°F (325°F convection) for 7–9 minutes. The cookies need to be pale brown all over, not whitish in the middle.

BAKING

The batter must always be spread as thinly and evenly as possible. Some pastry chefs make a stencil for themselves out of acetate, and use a spatula to scrape away excess batter, but I seem to get into a mess using this method (and of course the nuts get in the way for almond tuiles).

The cookies bake very quickly in the oven, so do not be tempted to bake too many at once—if you are starting out, it is a good idea to do a trial run of 4 or 5. Get everything ready for shaping before you bake, or you will run out of time.

Allow the baked cookies to cool on the tray for about 15 seconds, then nudge one with a small palette knife or spatula. At first it will seem as if it is not holding together, but be patient and it will soon become firm enough to handle. Now move quickly: slide your spatula underneath and shape it as you wish.

If the last of the cookies harden before you shape them, you have one more life. Put back in the oven for 1–2 minutes till soft again. I find you can do this only once before the cookies become brittle and impossible to shape.

For each new batch you will need to cool the baking tray and use fresh baking paper (or wash up your nonstick silicone mat with care).

SHAPING

The traditional shape is a tile shape. If you only make these occasionally you can lay the hot cookies over a rolling pin (no need to grease)—but I find the rolling pin follows its instincts and rolls, quite often breaking your cookies as it does so.

You can buy beautiful tuile molds, consisting of three or four concave channels in which to lay the cookies, but Peter came up with a far cheaper solution. He found a metre of unused PVC drainpipe and cut it down the center. I lay the cookies on the concave side, which is conveniently nonstick.

You do not of course have to stop at tuile shapes. To make an ice-cream cup, mould quickly into a small bowl or shallow ramekin, then transfer to a rack.

To make cigarettes, roll round the handle of a wooden spoon.

One of my favorite shapes is free-form twists, which take a bit of practice because the cookies are very hot to handle. Bake long thin fingers of batter (8x9½-inches long, about 1 inch wide). When beginning to go firm, pick up the hot cookie and wind round the handle of a wooden spoon into a corkscrew shape.

You can make tuile cones for mini cornets by crumpling foil into a cone shape and shaping a round cookie around it. You can also make striped or dotted tuiles or other shapes by mixing 1–2 tsp batter with cocoa, then dotting or piping over the tuile before baking, in the pattern that takes your fancy.

FORTUNE COOKIES

Make a fat-free batter (or else your fortunes will be greasy) from 1 egg white, few drops vanilla extract, pinch of salt, ¼ cup flour, 2½ tbsp sugar. Write or type out fortunes and fold into thin strips. Put 3 or 4 circles of batter 3½-inches in diameter on a very lightly greased baking sheet and bake at 400°F (same convection) for 4–6 minutes till golden round the edge, pale but dry in the center. Whip out of the oven, and as soon as the cookie is firm, invert on to a wooden board, put the fortune just below center and fold over the top, then immediately fold in quarter crosswise (like a pancake). As it cools it will try to unfold, so I pop them into mini-muffin cases to keep the shape.

Traditionally, each fortune should consist of a piece of advice or prediction (often cryptic), plus a lucky number. If you are stumped for fortunes, search the Internet under "fortune cookie fortunes."

Magnolia 'Nimbus', supplied by Spinners Nursery at Boldre in Hampshire, is my favorite plant in the whole garden—huge goblets fill the entire garden with scent for a whole month in early summer.

This incomparable recipe was delivered to my office in my *BBC Good Food* days by a colleague who worked at *Radio Times* upstairs—David Oppedisano. Like David, its origins are Boston, Massachusetts. The romantic name is explained by the cooking method—the cookies are left in the switched-off oven overnight.

Forgotten cookies

Makes about 30

2 egg whites

½ cup plus 1 tbsp golden superfine sugar

1 cup walnuts, roughly chopped (if you like extra crunch, toast them first: see page 236)

1 cup plus 2 tbsp 70% chocolate, roughly chopped

1 tsp vanilla extract

One guest renamed these as Never-to-be-Forgotten cookies.

Thoroughly heat the oven to 350°F (same temperature for convection)—it must be completely hot, not just up to temperature.

Whisk the egg whites with a good pinch of salt until stiff and dry. Gradually whisk in the sugar a little at a time to make a thick and glossy meringue. Tip in the nuts, chocolate and vanilla and gently fold in.

Line 2 baking sheets with foil. Spoon heaped teaspoonfuls (no larger) of the mixture, spaced apart, on to the sheets. Put in the oven and immediately turn the oven off. Leave without disturbing overnight.

In the morning, carefully peel the cookies from the foil and store in an airtight tin. Eat within a week.

After baking many batches of these cookies, we have found that occasionally, in humid weather, they do not cook through completely and the centers are sticky. If this happens, go back to the beginning—heat the oven, put in cookies, turn off oven. Check after 3 or 4 hours (or leave longer if convenient).

I love biscotti, but not when they are hard as dog biscuits and break your teeth unless dunked. These are crumbly, nutty and elegant enough to serve for dessert with a glass of Gaillac doux

Walnut-Armagnac biscotti

Makes about 50

⅔ cup walnuts

7 tbsp unsalted butter, softened

¾ cup plus 2 tbsp granulated sugar

2 eggs

1 tsp vanilla extract

1 tbsp Armagnac

2⅓ cups all-purpose flour

1½ tsp baking powder

Toast the walnuts in a 300°F (275°F convection) oven for 15–20 minutes, until they start to smell walnutty. Turn oven to 325°F (if using convection, leave at 275°F), and chop the nuts coarsely.

Cream the butter and sugar, beat in the eggs, then add the vanilla and Armagnac. In another bowl mix the flour, baking powder and ¼ tsp salt, and stir into the creamed mixture with the cooled nuts. On a large, lightly floured board, shape half the mixture into an even 12-inch-long log and roll it lumberjack-style but gently on to a baking sheet lined with parchment paper, so it lies diagonally (this gives it more space to spread). Repeat with the remaining mixture and another lined baking sheet.

Bake for 25–30 minutes; the dough will spread and should be lightly browned on top. Remove from the oven and cool for 5 minutes, then slide on to a board and slice obliquely about ⅓-inch thick. Lay the slices carefully back on baking sheets (you may need a third one at this stage) and bake for a further 15–20 minutes, till pale golden all over and crisp. Cool on the baking sheets then transfer to an airtight container.

When baking cookies, unless I need the baking sheets for another batch, I often disobey a golden rule of baking and leave them to cool on the sheet itself, as here. Once cooled they can then be transferred directly to the box or storage container, meaning one less manoeuver and fewer broken cookies.

RAYNAUDES SECRET

Toasted walnuts: we almost invariably toast walnuts before using them in recipes at Raynaudes—this enhances both flavor and crunch. If you are in a hurry you can toast them much more quickly—at 375°F (350°F convection)—but you will develop a better flavor at a lower temperature. The goes when toasting all other nuts, as does the rule that you should judge when they are toasted by nose, not eye.

Somewhere between a digestive cracker and an oatcake, this is the perfect foil for Comté, Roquefort, St-Marcellin, Langres and the other favorites on Peter's cheeseboard. They keep a fortnight in a tin if you can resist them.

Home-made Digestives

Makes 15–30, depending on size

1¼ cups medium oatmeal or rolled oats

1 cup whole wheat flour

3 tbsp plus 1 tsp brown sugar

5 tbsp butter

½ tsp baking soda

3–4 tbsp milk

squeeze of lemon juice

Process the first 3 ingredients till well combined. Add the butter, baking soda and ¼ tsp salt, then most of the milk and the lemon juice. Whiz till the mixture comes together, adding the remaining milk if necessary. The dough will be slightly tacky. Roll out on a floured surface to cracker thickness and stamp out rounds of whatever size you want. Making them small and elegant is harder work than making large ones. I have a 2-inch hexagonal cutter that gives a particularly attractive effect. Prick once or twice decoratively with a fork.

Bake at 400°F (375°F convection) for 10–12 minutes, till just starting to go brown at the edges, not all over. Smaller ones might take less time.

RAYNAUDES SECRET

The cheese board: crackers are only one option to serve alongside. The French like cheese plain, with a knife and fork and sometimes a little bread. We often accompany it with quince paste—a slab-like jam known in southern France as *cotignac* and in Spain as *membrillo*. (Making this is my least favorite kitchen procedure, as it spits burning jam all over the kitchen.)
From August, we often accompany cheese with grapes, first the 'Black Magic' variety from Sicily, later Muscat grapes from Moissac, north of Toulouse.

French toast is the great Manoir de Raynaudes breakfast treat. Although the principle of French toast, or *pain perdu*, is simply to dip bread in milk, this gives a much more delicious, crusty finish.

Raynaudes pain perdu

For 8 generous slices

3½ tbsp flour

2 tbsp granulated sugar

2 tsp vanilla extract

1 egg

1½ tbsp butter, melted (in the frying pan in which you will be making the French toast, to save washing up), plus more for frying

¾ cup milk

8 thick slices of brioche

TO SERVE

honey or maple syrup and wedges of lemon

Whisk the flour, sugar and a pinch of salt together in a wide bowl, then add the vanilla, egg, melted butter and milk. Whisk all together till smooth.

When ready to go, heat a little butter in the frying pan till good and hot—it should sizzle then the foam subside. Meanwhile, dip a slice of bread at a time in the egg mixture to immerse completely, then put in the pan. Cook without touching for 1½–2 minutes, till golden, then flip and cook the other side. Cook the other slices in the same way, two or three at once.

A Raynaudes breakfast-time favorite, packed with texture and flavor.

Tropical banana cake

Makes 2 cakes

15 tbsp unsalted butter, softened

1⅓ cups brown sugar

¾ cup plus 2 tbsp superfine sugar

2 eggs

1½ tsp vanilla

2 tbsp rum

4 very ripe bananas, mashed

3 cups all-purpose flour

1¼ tsp baking soda

½ tsp nutmeg

½ cup unsweetened coconut milk

1⅓ cup shredded unsweetened coconut

You will need two 9-inch round pans or two 8-inch square pans, buttered and floured

Using an electric mixer, cream the butter and sugars, then add the eggs, vanilla and rum. Add the bananas—the mixture will probably curdle.

Mix the flour, baking soda, nutmeg and ½ tsp salt, and add this to the banana mixture, with the machine still running, in batches, alternately with the coconut milk. Stir in the coconut and transfer to the pan or pans.

Bake at 350°F (325°F convection) for about 45 minutes until deep golden brown, slightly shrunk from the edge of pan and a skewer comes out clean from the center of the cake. Cool for 5 minutes in the pan then turn out.

This is a recipe for when you come across perfect summer apricots. It is what we call a "fresh" jam—to be kept in the fridge and eaten within ten days—and extremely quick and easy to make.

Fresh apricot jam

Makes 3 medium jars

2¼ pounds ripe apricots

1 cup plus 2 tbsp granulated sugar

Wash, halve and stone the fruit and cut each apricot into 6–8 small pieces. Put in a bowl and stir in the sugar, then leave in a cool place overnight.

Transfer to a preserving pan or large wide pan, bring slowly to a simmer, stirring often, and boil for 10–15 minutes, until it looks jammy. If you have a thermometer, you are aiming for 200°F (lower than conventional jam).

You can vary this recipe by adding a touch of fresh ginger at the first step, but do not overdo it

Homemade yogurt is much superior to bought. This is our most popular, and luxurious, flavor. We can buy vanilla powder from the spice lady in Carmaux market— it is made from powdered pods and gives a pleasing speckled surface to the yogurts.

Homemade vanilla yogurt

Makes 8 yogurts

1 gelatine leaf

⅓ cup evaporated (unsweetened) milk

2 tbsp skimmed-milk powder

3¾ cups whole milk

½ cup plain yogurt

TO FLAVOR

1 tsp vanilla extract

2–3 tbsp granulated sugar

pinch of vanilla powder (optional)

Soak the gelatine leaf in cold water while you assemble the other ingredients. Then squeeze out the leaf and put in a large measuring cup with the evaporated milk. Microwave for about 30 seconds, till the milk is hot and the gelatine has dissolved. Whisk well then stir in the skimmed-milk powder and about a quarter of the milk. Whisk again and stir in the yogurt, then the rest of the milk. At this point add the flavorings to taste.

Pour into the yogurt pots and follow machine directions. For our yogurt machine, this involves putting the lid on the machine (not on the pots themselves), pushing the button and leaving for 8 hours. Then removing pots, putting on lids and putting in the fridge. Not very difficult.

Make Your Own Yogurt

I have tried making yogurt in the airing cupboard, and by wrapping bowls in blankets, but we suffered the results rather than enjoyed them—until we invested in our *yaourtière*, an electric machine that simply warms the pots to a certain temperature for a certain time, then lets them slowly cool. We have rarely made a better investment. Homemade yogurt is pure, delicious and as healthy as what you put into it. It is now served every day at the Manoir breakfast, in an almost bewildering variety of flavors.

We do, however, have a secret. Having read the manual that came with the machine and two other French books on the subject, I was not satisfied. Most people do not want their yogurt runny; they prefer it very lightly set.

I experimented with gelatine and found that just one leaf gives a perfect soft set and prevents the runniness, or worse still stringiness, that homemade yogurt is famous for. For smoothness of flavor I also add some evaporated milk (in France you can buy handy 2⅔-ounce cans under the Gloria brand) and a little skimmed milk. For the rest of the milk, the safest option, at least if you want to keep the yogurt for more than one day, is sterilized, and full cream gives again the best flavor. As for the yogurt starter, I experimented with powder from the health food shop but found that adding a pot of readily available Danone Bio plain yogurt gave an identical result at a fraction of the cost. You could, of course, use a pot of yogurt from your last batch as a starter.

There, then, is our basic plain yogurt. When it comes to flavorings, the experiments became even more fascinating. My books suggested many weird and wonderful combinations, and the first flavor we ever served was verbena, made with a bright green liqueur called Verveine du Valay.

Since then I have tried over a dozen different flavors, some of which were never served, others have been met with acclaim. Here is what I have learned.

- Yogurt has quite a strong, sharp, clean flavor in its own right, so flavors added to it need to be quite assertive.

- For sweetened yogurts, I use 2–3 tbsp sugar per quarter of milk, which tastes a little too sweet when you pour it into the pots, but is correct when the yogurt has been made and chilled.

- Fruit yogurts are tricky. Fruit needs to be cooked or it will stop the yogurt setting, and it needs to be highly reduced or the flavor is weak. If you really want to make your own fruit yogurt, I suggest adding jam.

- Be aware that particles in the yogurt will float to the top, forming a crust. Vanilla and nutmeg look appealing, poppy seeds less so.

- Behind vanilla, our most popular flavors are rose (1 tbsp rose water, 2–3 tbsp sugar, 1–2 drops red or pink food coloring), honey (2 tbsp honey instead of the sugar), cinnamon (½ tsp freshly ground cinnamon, 2–3 tbsp sugar), lemon (½ tsp finely grated lemon zest infused in the milk and strained, 2–3 tbsp sugar).

At Raynaudes we make every breakfast as different as we can, including a choice of homemade muesli or granola. Of the various versions we make, this is probably the most popular. Measuring the ingredients in a mug—about 1 cup capacity—speeds things up.

Honey almond granola

PUT IN A BIG BOWL

4 mugs rolled oats

1 mug oat bran (or ordinary bran)

2 mugs whole unskinned almonds, roughly chopped

PUT IN A LARGE PITCHER

1 mug skimmed-milk powder

¾ mug sunflower oil

¾ mug honey

1 tbsp vanilla extract

½ tsp salt

few drops of almond extract (*see* Raynaudes Secret, below)

ADD WHEN COLD

1 mug raisins, chopped dates or other dried fruit

You will need 2 rimmed baking sheets or roasting pans, lightly greased

Mix the oats and nuts. Whisk the milk powder and liquids then pour over the oats and mix thoroughly, either with a big spoon or your hands. Transfer to baking sheets and bake at 325°F (275°F convection) for 20 minutes. Stir well, switch the lower and upper pans so they cook evenly, and bake for another 15–25 minutes, till the oats are golden and the nuts look nicely toasted. The granola will crisp as it cools. Stir in raisins when cold. Serve with milk.

MAKE IT LOOK GREAT

Granola looks best served in a tall glass jar. Store it somewhere completely airtight and it will keep up to 10 days.

RAYNAUDES SECRET

Many almond extracts are harsh and synthetic, so go easy. I have found a good natural extract and use up to ½ tsp. When visiting Agen, France's prune capital north of Toulouse, I encountered a wonderful scented oil made from plum kernels (*huile vierge d'amandons de pruneaux*). It adds a haunting fragrance to dishes—I use about 2 tbsp in this recipe (reducing the sunflower oil accordingly). It is also good in dressings or to drizzle over warm salads.

At Raynaudes we serve the sort of breakfast we would like to eat if we were on holiday: fresh, light, indulgent—plus almost invariably, a surprise. One of the best surprises has to be our smoothie—an icy cup of lipstick-pink goodness.

The Raynaudes smoothie

Makes enough for 6

2 ripe bananas

2 tbsp honey

2 cups plain yogurt

½ cup apple juice

2 cups raspberries, frozen
(or mangoes, or other fruit)

Whiz everything in a blender till smooth. (Powerful as a food processor is, its blades work in a different way from a blender, and you get a much smoother effect with the latter.) Taste and add more honey if necessary, and more fruit juice if too thick. Serve at once, though it will still be delicious half an hour later.

RAYNAUDES SECRET

Fresh juice at breakfast is a worthy destination for the luscious fruit that drop from our twenty-one espaliered trees from August to October, faster than we can collect them. To stop the juice going brown, we often cut up a grapefruit or pomegranate (no need to peel) and juice it with the rest.

The Manoir address book

It has taken us four years of trial and error to find the best suppliers in the area – all of these offer exceptional quality and service.

ALBY FOIE GRAS: paradise for *foie gras* fans. Everything ducky, fresh or vac-packed or tinned, plus cute gifts such as *foie gras* spoons, mini-terrines and "duckanters" for pouring the obligatory accompanying glass of sweet white. Rue Lévizac, 81000 ALBI TEL 0563 60 74 82 (also in Albi covered market)

BIO-AZUR: more than a health food store – a gourmet paradise of rare oils, exotic dried fruits and seeds and grains sold loose. If you spot the Statue of Liberty as you fly round the *rocade*, Bio-Azur is just behind it. 281 rue Roc, 81000 ALBI TEL 0563 54 52 57

CARMAUX MARKET: Friday 8 a.m. until noon. The real thing – knocks spots off other markets in the area. Best stalls: in Jean-Jaurès – Yannick (fruit). In Gambetta – the two Christians (cheese), Le Pic (goat's cheese), Gayraud (fish). In rue de l'Hôtel de Ville – Campos (poultry), Mitou (olives), The Spice Lady, Serge Sabatier (mushrooms). For meat, head up the road to M. Rul (right)

MICHELE CAVAILLÉ: makes the authentic *pastis du Quercy*, an extraordinary and show-stopping apple tart made with strudel pastry coiled into a sort of giant turban. You can buy Mme Cavaillé's *pastis* at Montauban and Caylus markets (Tarn-et-Garonne) but best to order. 82240 LAVAURETTE TEL 0563 64 95 46

CAVE MADER: when not buying direct from the vineyard, we shop at M. Mader's friendly emporium in the Place Jean Jaurès, Carmaux. (The ornamental ducks on our lake were a gift from Mme Mader.) 19 Place Jean Jaurès, 81400 CARMAUX TEL 0563 36 83 00

CBP: ignore the fact they do not put the lights on, this is kit heaven if you like baking and pastry work.

Baskets for proving baguettes, chocolate dipping forks, Bollywood-style wedding cake decs. No credit cards. 10 rue Sérieyssols, 81000 ALBI TEL 05 63 54 52 82

MICHEL CLUIZEL: every mouthful of chocolate that is eaten at the Manoir comes from the Normandy chocolatier. Our favourite is the complex, almost smoky Vila Gracinda from the island of São Tomé off the Nigerian coast. Michel Cluizel, Avenue de Conches, 27240 DAMVILLE TEL 0232 35 60 00, www.cluizel.com

EFIMS: the steel and pine pergola that dominates the Manoir garden was designed and built by metal specialist Xavier Giendaj. Ingenious and affordable. 28 Grand Chemin, 81400 LABISTIDE GABAUSSE TEL 0563 54 23 73, efims.be@wanadoo.fr

L'EPICURIEN: if you go to only one restaurant in the Tarn, enjoy the confident, suave, up-to-the-minute cooking from Swedish chef Rickard. 42 Place Jean Jaurès, 81000 ALBI TEL 0563 53 10 70

LA FLEURÉE DE PASTEL: before violets, the wealth of Toulouse was built on woad (*pastel*) and this shop celebrates its revival, with everything you can think of (scarves, shirts, ink, artists' paints, emulsion) in the characteristic rich, luminous, noble shade of blue. Suppliers of the woad-tinted wax that seals the corks of the Manoir's *eau-de-vie de cérises*. Hôtel Pierre Delfau, 20 rue de la Bourse, 31000 TOULOUSE TEL 0561 12 05 94, www.bleu-de-lectoure.com

LES FRERES BRASSEURS: local brewer. For a soft Belgian-style beer choose *Tolosa* "Bière Cathare." Payssel, 81400 BLAYES LES MINES TEL 0563 36 87 80

JARDIN DES BASTIDES: Sylvie Gravier runs a fine nursery, as well as being an accomplished garden designer and landscaper. La Ségalar, 81170 MILHARS TEL 0563 56 36 61

LEGUMES DU LUGANIE: enthusiastic young couple with organic smallholding at neighbouring village of Trévien. Vegetable box scheme. TEL 0689 81 03 05

AU MARCHÉ D'ORIENT: North African ingredients, teas and spices. Opposite Géant supermarket, 11 allée Camping, 81000 ALBY TEL 0563 45 05 69

MONESTIÈS STORES: the ultimate village shop. Bernard's van (known as Aladdin's Cave) combs the local byways offering slippers, pot plants, fine cheeses, besoms, plastic poker chips and everything in between. Place de la Poste, 81640 MONESTIÈS TEL 0563 76 11 51

MORIN MAREE: take the Stade/Ecole des Mines turn-off on the Albi *rocade* (bypass). Funky trawler-shaped shopfront conceals a palace for fish lovers: live lobsters, samphire, three sorts of smoked salmon, plus every fish you can think of. 13 ave Mendès France, 81000 ALBI TEL 0563 38 72 58

MOULIN DE MONTRICOUX: it took two years to track down really good plain and strong flour in the region. Montricoux is a small town among the bastide villages of Penne and Bruniquel, about an hour from the Manoir. We use Montricoux's *Farine de tradition* for plain, *Gruau* for bread. Minimum 5kg. 82800 MONTRICOUX TEL 0563 67 21 51

MOULIN PATISSERIE: strategically placed near Cordes-sur-Ciel market in the lower town, the best *patissier* in the Tarn. Outstanding *sablés* (chocolate or praline biscuit squares), *viennoiseries* (croissants, brioches), *gâteaux* and *choux*. M. Moulin's *croquembouche* makes an amazing centrepiece for a wedding. Place de la Bouteillerie, 81170 CORDES-SUR-CIEL TEL 0563 56 00 41

OFIR ASIASS ASSOCIATES: young Tel Aviv architect who masterminded renovation of Le Manoir. Special talents: indoor–outdoor living, blending ancient and modern. oasiass@bzeqint.net

PERLES DE GASCOGNE: producer of an esoteric oil made from the kernels of plum stones, used to scent almond dishes at the Manoir. You can contact the farm direct on TEL 0553 70 21 55, but they will tell you to go to Agen covered market to track down (expensive) 25cl bottles of *Huile vierge d'amandons de pruneaux.*

LA ROSERAIE DU DESERT: we spent many months searching for good advice on roses, and found it west of Toulouse at John and Becky Hook's excellent rose nursery. They selected and supplied all the roses at the Manoir. Panjas, 32290 BOUZON GELLENAVE TEL 0562 09 15 46, www.frenchtearose.com

BERNARD RUL: friendly local butcher, immaculate little shop, especially strong on pork and veal. Carmaux's best-kept secret. 30 ave Jean Baptiste Calvignac, 81400 CARMAUX TEL 0563 76 53 29

TARN VIANDE: Albi's best butcher. Be prepared to queue, and take a woolly (fierce air conditioning). 6 rue Hippolyte Crozes, 81000 ALBI TEL 0563 46 21 17, www.tarnviande.fr

LE MANOIR DE RAYNAUDES: in 2007 we opened our 'shop', two glass-fronted cabinets near the piano. All our gifts and treats are exclusive to the Manoir, and include lavender oil and water distilled from our own 'Maillette' lavender, prints of Libby Edmondson's "Le Manoir" and "Le Potager," postcards, a small range of our own preserves and condiments and greetings cards handmade using Manoir fabrics. We also do a nice line in *chambres d'hôtes*, apartments and dinners. Le Manoir de Raynaudes, 81640 MONESTIÈS TEL 0563 36 91 90, www.raynaudes.com.

Notes for cooks

Butter

Unsalted butter is the norm in France and where I think it is important to use unsalted I have specified. However, most cooks will work out for themselves that you can use lightly salted or salted butter if you decrease the salt in the rest of the recipe. For information, unsalted butter freezes better than salted.

Eggs

The recipes in this book have been tested using large eggs. Medium eggs weigh around 21 ounces, large 24 ounces (potential difference 0–37 per cent, average 19 per cent), so you can judge for yourself whether using a medium egg will materially alter a recipe.

Yeast

I use fresh yeast, which is well worth the small trouble of seeking out. If you have not used fresh yeast – available freely nowadays from supermarket bakery sections and health shops – I strongly recommend it. I find it more reliable and quicker to rise than dried, the dough has more bounce and the finished bread seems somehow more fragrant. If you use dried yeast, it will work for all these recipes, but use half the weight of dried to fresh, and check the packet to see whether it is the type that should be dissolved in liquid, or added direct to flour. If it says dissolve in liquid, follow the instructions and timing suggested. Dried yeast generally takes a little longer to work than fresh, so take this into account. More about breadmaking on page 220.

Fan Ovens

Many cookery writers are frightened of giving fan oven temperatures, but as most cooks now use fan ovens, and the manufacturers are keen to standardize their products, I have given the temperatures I use in my domestic Neff fan oven. Sometimes my indications differ from the 70°F reduction suggested in my oven handbook, and in one case I suggest not using the fan oven setting at all (Lemon pot de crème, page 176). Two other comments for fan-oven users: we are told it is unnecessary to preheat fan ovens, but unless it is a very long slow session in the oven, I disagree. And to get things evenly baked, I do find it helps to switch baking trays or turn things round during the baking process.

Measuring spoons

In my experience, the most common cause of failure in baking is not using proper measuring spoons. Teaspoons (5ml) and tablespoons (15ml) are the same in Britain and in the US. Australian cooks note that an Australian tablespoon (20ml) is larger than the British, so for a tablespoon in this book measure 3 tsp instead.

American cups

Increasingly, American cooks are investing in scales, which (although fiddly) make measuring more accurate. If using American cups, here are the most common translations.

Butter	225g	1 cup/2 sticks
Cheese, grated	125g	1 cup
Flour	150g	1 cup
Nuts, chopped	125g	1 cup
Rice	200g	1 cup
Sugar	200g	1 cup

Oven temperatures

CELSIUS	FAHRENHEIT	GAS
110	225	¼
130	250	½
140	275	1
150	300	2
160	325	3
180	350	4
190	375	5
200	400	6
220	425	7
230	450	8
240	475	9

Volume

15ml	½fl oz
30ml	1fl oz
50ml	2fl oz
100ml	3½fl oz
120ml	4fl oz
150ml	5fl oz (¼ pint)
200ml	7fl oz (⅓ pint)
225ml	8fl oz (1 cup US)
250ml	9fl oz (1 cup Australian)
300ml	10fl oz (½ pint)
450ml	15fl oz (¾ pint)
500ml	18fl oz
1 liter	1¾ pints (1 quart US)
1.2 liters	2 pints

Weight

10g	¼oz
15g	½oz
25g	1oz
50g	1¾oz
75g	2¾oz
100g	3½oz
150g	5½oz
175g	6oz
200g	7oz
225g	8oz (½lb)
250g	9oz
275g	9¾oz
300g	10½oz
350g	12oz (¾lb)
375g	13oz
400g	14oz
425g	15oz
450g	1lb
500g	1lb 2oz
700g	1½lb
750g	1lb 10oz
1kg	2¼lb
1.25kg	2lb 12oz
1.5kg	3lb 5oz
2kg	4½lb
2.25kg	5lb
2.5kg	5lb 5oz
3kg	6½lb

Measurement

3mm	⅛ in
5mm	¼ in
1cm	½ in
2cm	¾ in
2.5cm	1 in
3cm	1¼ in
4cm	1½ in
4.5cm	1½ in
5cm	2 in
7.5cm	3 in
10cm	4 in
12cm	4½ in
15cm	6 in
18cm	7 in
20cm	8 in
23cm	9 in
25cm	10 in
30cm	12 in

Index

Acknowledgements

The making of this book has been both exciting and harmonious. My most important thank you is to Vivien Bowler at Harper Collins for having dreamed up and commissioned *A Table in the Tarn*. If she ever fancies a career change, she also proved herself a highly creative stylist for the photography. Mari Roberts made the editing process a fascinating pleasure, and improved this book in a thousand ways. My agent Fiona Lindsay and Mary Bekheit provided support and encouragement over a year of writing and rewriting.

It was a delight to work with photographer Jonathan Buckley, whose pictures of the Manoir, its food and surroundings bring our story so brilliantly to life. (Even before being published here, his orchid picture on page 161 has won the Garden Writers Guild's 'Single Image of the Year' award.) Special thanks too to the Manoir's assistant chef Caro Garman for her skilful food styling. I would like to thank Andrew Barron for casting his art directorial spell over the design of this book, and for transforming our words and pictures with such skill and imagination.

Recipes are not born from thin air, and I have many sources to thank for the ideas you will find in *A Table in the Tarn*. Top of my reading list each month remain *BBC Good Food* and *Olive* magazines, which between them cover every imaginable aspect of the British food scene. Another enduring source of inspiration and knowledge comes from across the Atlantic in the form of two magazines – *Cook's Illustrated* (and its website) and *Fine Cooking*, which never fail to deliver exciting, exhaustively tested recipes and inspiration.

Looking over my shoulder, as it were, I am always aware of two food gurus who taught me more about cooking and recipe writing than everyone else put together. They were my colleagues for six happy years at *BBC Good Food*, and now they are friends – Mary Cadogan and Angela Nilsen.

The Manoir kitchen has space for only three slim shelves of cookery books. They are dog-eared because I use them every day, and many of the recipes and ideas in this book are inspired by and adapted from them: Paula Wolfert, *The Cooking of South West France*; Alice Waters, *Chez Panisse Cooking*, *Chez Panisse Desserts*, *Chez Panisse Vegetables*, *Chez Panisse Café Cookbook*; Jeanne Strang, *Goose Fat and Garlic*; Judy Rodgers, *The Zuni Café Cookbook*; Dan Lepard and Richard Whittington, *Baking with Passion*; Raymond Blanc, *Foolproof French*; *Leith's Bible*; Molly Stevens, *All About Braising*; Dorie Greenspan, *Baking* and *Chocolate Desserts with Pierre Hermé*; *The Joy of Cooking*; Ruth Rogers and Rose Gray, *The River Café Cookbook*.

In the Manoir office I have many more shelves of cookbooks, where my other heroes reside. I would like to specifically thank the writers who have directly inspired recipes or techniques in this book, namely: Celia Brooks-Brown, Stephen Bull, the late Robert Carrier, Barney Desmazery, Ursula Ferrigno, Brian Glover, the late Jane Grigson, Nigella Lawson, Emily Lucchetti, the late Richard Olney, David Oppedisano, Thane Prince, Brigid Roberson, Michel Roux, Delia Smith, Ruth Watson, Anne Willan.

Peter and I would like to thank local friends Trevor and Sue Lowndes (official seamstress to the Manoir), Ali and Bjørn Christiansen, Bridget and Peter Dixon for their kindness and unfailing support since arriving in the area. We would be lost without designer Sue Miller, who created the Manoir's logo, branding and innumerable pieces of stationery, and World Archipelago, who designed our website (www.raynaudes.com). Not to mention all the other friends, family, neighbours and colleagues who have helped us turn the Raynaudes dream into reality.

Finally, the secret ingredient of any stay at Le Manoir is our guests themselves, who bring the place alive and make our life here a delight. We would specially like to mention a particularly loyal few: Adrian and Pauline Phillips, Adrian Pyne and Gordon McKenzie, Cameron and Greg Munro, Charles and Gabrielle Battersby, Danny and Gill Rowley, Ian, Virginia and Ellie McArdle, Ian and Isabel Orr, Iain and Yvonne Morton, Jean and Tony Welch, Jilly Sitford and Martin Topping, Kevin and Julia Regan, Leila Witkin, Mark and Anne Templeman, Mike and Mary Ambler, Nigel and Libby Edmondson, Paul Steggall and Shameem Sangha, Peter and Lynne Roberts, Ray and Karen Lewis, Ruth and David Watson, Sheila and Jimmy Skardon, Simon and Lyndsey Welch, Tony and Margaret Benson, Victoria and Ashley McNeil, Wendy and Pat Allott – plus the never-to-be-forgotten Colin and Carole Gregg and family.